# Teaching. . .
# Take This Job & Love It!

## Jerry King

Insight Publishing Company
Sevierville, Tennessee

Insight Publishing Company
1142 Dolly Parton Parkway
Sevierville, TN 37862

Published in Sevierville, Tennessee by Insight Publishing Company.

This book contains information gathered from many sources. the publisher and author disclaim any personal liability, either directly or indirectly, for advice or information presented within. Although the authors and publisher have used care and diligence in the presentation, and made every effort to ensure the accuracy and completeness of the information contained in this book, we assume no responsibility for errors, inaccuracies, omissions, or any inconsistency herein. Any slights of people, places, publishers, books, or organizations are unintentional.

First Printing 2001
Second and Third Printing 2003
ISBN No. 1-885640-77-3
Library of Congress cataloging—in Publication data

## ATTENTION SCHOOLS, EDUCATIONAL ORGANIZATIONS AND EDUCATORS:

Quantity discounts are available on bulk purchases of this book. Special Customized Editions can also be created to fit specific needs. For information, please contact our Special Sales Department at 1142 Dolly Parton Parkway, Sevierville, TN 37862 or call (865) 429-0252.

# Dedication

**This book is dedicated to my wife, Lucy:**

This book—and my life—would be impossible without your unfailing love, patience, support, and faith in me. You "teach" me what is truly important in life. . .unconditional loving relationships!

**My sons, Jon and Chris:**

I am so proud of what you guys have become, who you are, and your unlimited potential in the future. You "teach" me not to sweat the small stuff in life and to have fun—even at my old age!

**This book is in memory of:**

My sister, Ronda King, whose courageous fight with Lupus, and my mother, Stella King, whose hard-fought battle with cancer ended in victory. You both "taught" me that laughter really is the best medicine during life's difficult times and that living a life of significance is more important than any "success" on earth!

# Thanks!

I sincerely appreciate each person who contributed, directly or indirectly, to the completion of one of my biggest goals and dreams...writing a book to help teachers achieve success in their personal and professional lives!

Thanks to every person whose research, work or publication was used as a resource.

Thanks to the wonderful people at Insight Publishing Company. A special "thank you" to David Wright, President, for his professional and personal assistance from the beginning to the end of this project. Also, Brent Sapp and Barbara Goggans for their hard work and long hours in editing the manuscript.

Thanks to Sandy Worrell for her outstanding photography expertise used for the cover. Also, to Douglas Graphics for the cover design.

Thanks to God, my Creator, for giving me the opportunity to learn from so many dedicated "teachers" from all walks of life!

# Table Of Contents

## STAGE I

## STAGE II

## STAGE III

# To All Schoolteachers

YOU are the most influential people in the world!

YOU are the true heroes of our time!

YOU make a positive difference in the lives of young people every day!

YOU plant the seeds of greatness!

I hope the information in this book will help you continue the positive, life-changing job you do and lead you further on life's exciting journey of success for yourself, your family and your students.

God bless you!

"My father and mother wanted me to be a brain surgeon, but I exceeded all their expectations. . .
I BECAME A TEACHER!"

*Harry K. Wong*


The mediocre teacher tells.
The good teacher explains.
The superior teacher demonstrates.
The great teacher inspires.

*William Arthur Ward*

# A New Day for Teachers!

This is the beginning of a new day! God has given me this day to use as I will. I'm a teacher, motivator of learning and builder of foundations. I can waste today or use it for good. I can go to school prepared and enthusiastic or grumble about my job and its many responsibilities. I can look at it as a challenge to grow or just another long day to get through.

What I do today is important, because I am exchanging one day of my life for it. I can never go back and re-do it. . .so I have to get it right the first time - to understand sympathetically, to listen sincerely, to share openly, to teach creatively. . .to do my best!

When tomorrow comes, this day will be gone forever, leaving in its place something that I have traded for it. It was my decision and my choice that shaped my attitude and actions today. I want this day to be a gain, not loss; good, not evil; success, not failure; in order that I shall not regret the high price I paid for today.

I want to say at the end of today, "I succeeded in reaching my students; I showed an earnest concern for others and helped my class grow in knowledge and self-esteem."

I invested one whole day of my life and I need to know it was worthwhile; it counted for something special. It was a good day and tomorrow can even be better!

Adapted by Lana Eckard

Most of us end up with no more than five or six people who remember us. Teachers have thousands of people who remember them for the rest of their lives.

Andy Rooney, Journalist

# Teacher Success Strategy 1

## UNLEASH YOUR PERSONAL POWER WITH A DYNAMIC SELF-IMAGE!

**YOU! Yes—YOU. . .are a unique, one-of-a-kind person who was born to be a winner in the classroom and in life!** You have unlimited potential to become the person you were meant to be! The fact that you opened this book is evidence you want more out of life than you currently get. You've taken the first and most important step toward *making your dreams become a reality*!

As a teacher, you experience unprecedented stress, responsibilities, and a weekly grind that probably includes faculty meetings, parent-teacher meetings, preparing and grading tests, bus duty, cafeteria duty, game duty, committee meetings, preparing lesson plans, in-service meetings, averaging grades, and did I mention—*more meetings*?

1

On many nights do you, like thousands of other teachers, turn the lights off, pull the covers to your chin, exhale with a big sigh and think, "Is this it? Is this what teaching, (and life), are all about?" If you feel like you're on the treadmill of life and don't know how to get off, this book was written for *you*! If you feel overworked, underpaid, unappreciated, and unfulfilled in your personal and professional life, this book was written for *you*. And if you're currently experiencing a mountaintop high in your life, this book is also for you. You will get even *more* out of life.

Are you optimistic about your future? Have your dreams become a reality? One of the saddest situations in life is when our dreams become regrets. Regardless of your current situation at school and home, remember:

> **When your dreams are big enough,**
> **the facts don't count!**

Each of us has dreams. As teachers, we all want to believe we have a special gift to make a difference in young people's lives. We all want to touch others in a special way. At some point we all see ourselves experiencing a high quality of life—living our dreams. Yet, for many of us those dreams have become as blurred as wearing dirty contact lenses. The frustrations and routines of daily life, at school and at home, cause us to give up the dreams we cherished at the beginning of our teaching career. That's when we start looking for the greener grass in another profession.

But wait a minute! I have great news for you! There's more to life—without changing jobs! There's hope for you to live the fulfilling life you were created to live! There is hope for YOU and your teaching career.

> **When there is hope for the future,
> there is power in the present.**
>
> **Dr. John C. Maxwell**

Susan was born in severe poverty, too embarrassed to go to elementary school because she only had one dress. But, *she had big dreams and hopes.* She earned her Ph.D. in education and became a leading university professor.

Jim was so obese he had to lose over 170 pounds before he could buckle his seatbelt. He hated every minute of every day as a teacher. But, *he had big dreams and hopes.* He lost the weight; then he started a wellness and exercise class for teachers at his school. Two years later, a more confident Jim was recognized for his enthusiasm and love for children as he was named Teacher of the Year.

Juanita was physically and sexually abused as a teen. She dropped out of high school. She swore she could never trust anyone enough to share a loving relationship. But, *she also had big dreams and hopes.* She eventually received her high school and college diplomas, married the man of her dreams, and started an enormously successful school-counseling program.

Just like these people and thousands of others, **YOU** have the same **Personal Power** within you. Personal Power simply means you have the ability to **take action**!

Research reveals that of the 100 most successful people in the world 70% overcame poverty, abuse, or a physical handicap. These people attributed their success to the challenges and obstacles they conquered. What challenges do you need to conquer in your class-room, and more importantly—in your life?

**If you don't have a plan for your life, someone else does.**

**Do you have a success plan for your personal and professional life?** If not, this handbook for teachers is **your** blueprint for success!

Think of a movie you liked so much you watched it more than once. Why did you watch it again? Each time you watched the movie, did it end the same way? Of course it did. Most teachers want different results, or a different ending to "their movie," but think they can keep doing the same thing. **You must <u>change</u> your thoughts, beliefs, and actions if you want different results**. Griping about situations in your personal life or about your job as a teacher won't bring different results. It takes a positive plan of action.

**If you keep doin' what you've been doin', you're gonna keep gettin' what you've got!**

**This book includes a proven success plan for YOU!** If you're not satisfied with different areas of your life, you must *<u>change</u>* your game plan. This book will help you get the results you want!

Have you looked at your high school yearbook lately? One glance will relinquish any doubts you have about how much you and your classmates have changed. Nice haircut, by the way, and how about those clothes?

Remember the Hula Hoop, Slinky, and Silly Putty? Even though they are still sold in stores, they're no longer hot items. Why? Times, people, needs, and wants change.

Need proof that schools have changed from what they used to be? Read the following list of teacher responsibilities in 1915:

# Rules of Conduct for Teachers
## (Board Of Education School Bulletin, 1915)

1. You will not marry during the terms of your contract.

2. You are not to keep company with men.

3. You must be home between the hours of 8:00 p.m. and 6:00 a.m. unless attending a school function.

4. You may not loiter in downtown ice cream stores.

5. You may not travel beyond city limits unless you have permission of the chairman of the board.

6. You may not ride in a carriage or automobile with any man, unless he is your father or brother.

7. You may not smoke cigarettes.

8. You may not dress in bright colors.

9. You may under no circumstances dye your hair.

10. You must wear at least two petticoats.

11. Your dresses must not be any shorter than two inches above your ankles.

12. To keep the schoolroom neat and clean, you must sweep the floor at least once a week with hot, soapy water; clean the blackboards at least once a day; and start the fire by 7:00 a.m. so the room will be warm by 8:00 a.m.

During my elementary school years I lived in South Carolina. I remember how hot the pavement felt when I ran barefooted across the street during those scorching summers. I screamed when my feet touched the sizzling asphalt, then smiled with relief as the pain disappeared. Like running across hot pavement, change sometimes causes temporary discomfort and pain in our lives. And if we give in to the burn of that pain, we'll soon *freeze* into a state of fear and apathy. Successful teachers aren't satisfied to stand in the middle of mediocrity. Average just isn't acceptable to great teachers.

To get more out of your life, you must be willing to take risks, deal with the temporary pain of change when it comes, and break out of your *comfort zone* with every ounce of energy you possess. Face it: if you wait until every situation is right, you'll wait forever.

> **Accept the challenges so that you may feel the
> exhilaration of victory.**
>
> **General George S. Patton**

Change and challenge are bound together like the strands of a cord. If you want to experience the exhilaration of victory in your classroom, you must break through the boundaries of your comfort zone by changing your emotional frame of mind. Three emotions can prevent you from fully enjoying your teaching career, as well as the rest of your life. These feelings combine to form what we'll call the "FUD Factor"—Fear, Uncertainty, and Doubt. We all wrestle with them. So let's be honest with each other. I'm not particularly fond of riding roller coasters. Let me rephrase that; I get sweaty palms waiting in line to ride Dumbo at Disney World.

Fear, uncertainty, and doubt inhibit your success by reducing your level of self-confidence. So what kind of fear do you face in your classroom:

- Fear of embarrassment when a student asks a question you can't answer?
- Fear of losing control of the classroom?
- Fear of teaching a difficult subject?
- Fear of technology as a teaching tool?
- Fear of your principal—especially when she/he visits unannounced?

FUDs can keep you from becoming the highly successful teacher and person you can be.

**Important Question:**
**What if you knew you only had one day left to live?**
**That day is tomorrow.**

Would you do anything differently? Who would you visit or call? Let's apply the same premise to your profession as a teacher: if you *had* to teach tomorrow—your last day on earth—what would you do differently? Would you treat everyone at school the same as usual—students, teachers, administrators, staff—as if it were just another day? How would you want these people to remember you on your last day?

If your thinking and behavior would change for the better because it's your last day, then why not change. . .right now! Don't put off beginning your journey of success.

A painfully shy man once fell deeply in love with a young woman. He sensed she felt the same way, but he couldn't find the courage to ask her out for a date. Finally, he decided he would mail her a love letter every day for one year, and then ask her out for a date.

He faithfully followed his plan, and at the end of the year he drummed up the courage to call her—only to find out she had married the mailman! Don't procrastinate! *Procrastination if one of the leading killers of success.*

To benefit most from this book, you will need to do more than just *read* it. I'm going to ask you to *do* this book. Your new journey of success begins with your honest, personal affirmation of your decision to *change* and get more out of life than you're currently getting. Please complete the Success Activities, and don't hesitate to underline or highlight any important points or quotes.

First of all, let's agree to what I refer to as the *3 Gottas.* Please re-write each statement on the line following it to affirm your decision to change.

**I gotta. . .be open to new possibilities**

_____

**I gotta. . .be committed to action!**

_____

**I gotta. . .break out of my comfort zone!**

_____

My apology if you are an English teacher. I am well aware that gotta is slang and the word *burst* is more appropriate than *bust,* but I will take advantage of writer's freedom. Also, I write on the seventh grade, third month level. . .so school administrators and college professors can understand what I am trying to say. Just kidding! I'm appreciative and thankful for school administrators' sense of humor—especially those in the school divisions where I've enjoyed the privilege of teaching.

I love the following story. A school administrator shared it with me:

A man in a hot air balloon realized he was lost. He reduced altitude and spotted a woman below. He descended a bit more and shouted, "Can you help me? I promised a friend I'd meet him an hour ago, but I don't know where I am."

The woman replied, "You're in a hot air balloon hovering about 30 feet above the ground, between 40 and 41 degrees north latitude, and between 59 and 60 degrees west longitude."

"You must be a teacher," said the balloonist. "I am," replied the women, "but how did you know?"

8

"Well," answered the man, "everything you told me is technically correct, but I have no idea what to make of your information, and the fact is, I'm still lost. Frankly, you haven't been much help to me so far."

The teacher responded, "You must be a school administrator." "I am," replied the balloonist, "but how did you know that?" "Well," said the woman, "you don't know where you are or where you are going. You have risen to where you are due to a lot of hot air. You made a promise which you have no idea how to keep, and you expect ME to solve your problem. The fact is, sir, you're in exactly the same position you were in before we met, but now, somehow it's MY fault."

### Teachers are real people, too—almost.

During my first year of teaching one of my students saw me pushing my cart through the grocery store. After scanning the cart contents, full of the junk food items of my typical shopping spree— Dr. Pepper, doughnuts, chips and dip, and three half-gallons of ice cream—she exclaimed, "Wow, Mr. King, I guess teachers are real people, too—almost." As a teacher, standing in front of your class, did it ever occur to you that many of your students don't even consider you a *real human being?*

I speak and present at many educator conferences and in-service training programs throughout the country. I've rarely observed any training that equips teachers to experience a successful *personal life.* As a teacher, you'll experience success *in* the classroom only if you experience success *outside* the classroom.

As often as educators try to separate the two, it's impossible to do. I've read the same book you have, telling us to leave our personal problems at home. That's one of those concepts that looks good on paper, but just won't work in the real world of teaching. If you're stressed out about a relationship or situation in your personal life, can it affect your performance in the classroom? Of course it can, and it will control you if you allow it to. Strategy #3 for Highly Successful Teachers specifically deals with how you can successfully manage teacher stress and burnout.

The first three strategies directly pertain to your personal life. To include only classroom strategies would be unfair to you and your students. For you to experience success at school, you must first be successful in your personal life - beginning with improving your self-image.

**Successful people become successful teachers!**

This book has absolutely no value to you unless you apply the strategies, not just read them. Even the number one success book in the world, the Bible, will not change you until you practice its powerful success principles.

**Halloween is over. You can take your mask off.**

How many times have you heard that statement from students the day after Halloween? (Actually, they say it to me all year). These success strategies will make a positive difference in your life only to the extent you *apply them* and are honest with yourself. This is not Halloween. No masks allowed. When you discover the truth about yourself, you'll experience more energy and enthusiasm than you ever imagined possible, both in the classroom and at home!

The age-old wisdom, *you reap what you sow*, is still true.

- Sow a seed—Reap a reward.
- Sow indifference in the classroom—Reap students who don't care about school or your class.
- Sow disorganization and no preparation—Reap classroom discipline problems.
- Sow disrespect and impatience at home—Reap broken relationships.
- Sow enthusiasm in the classroom—Reap motivated students who complete their assignments.
- Sow preparation—Reap students who don't have time to become discipline problems.
- Sow love and patience at home—Reap more loving, lasting personal relationships.

***Are you satisfied with what you reap?*** If not, I encourage you to *change* what you sow. . .beginning right now! Remember: in order to *have* the things you want, you must be the right kind of person and *do* the right things. Sow these proven teacher success strategies and you'll reap a positive, fulfilling life you never thought possible!

You must answer the same question coaches ask their teams during half-time of a close game: **how badly do you want it?** Or, as I heard an Arkansas preacher once say, "You gotta have the *want to*."

Do you have the want to? Do you really want to be the most effective and successful teacher you can possibly be? Elie Wiesel, Nobel Peace Prize winner once stated, "The opposite of success is not failure, it's indifference." There's no room for indifference in successful teaching.

You must want it badly enough to apply these success strategies and make a 100% commitment to apply them every day. I challenge anyone to convince a couple, married happily for 20 years or more, to attribute their success to a 50% effort. Both people had to make a 100% commitment— not 50/50! Success requires commitment, com-

commitment requires sacrifice, and sacrifice usually requires—brace yourself—change.

You don't need to give your life for success, but you must be willing to make changes necessary to get the results you want.

Remember, if you want different results in your personal and professional life, you must decide to *do* something different - not just *read* about it in this book.

*The 6 Dynamic Strategies of Highly Successful Teachers* can get you out of the rut of life we all experience at one time or another. Someone asked me the difference between a rut and a grave. I said, "About 6 inches!" Living our lives in a humdrum *rut* keeps us from enjoying life and loving the people we care about most.

Whenever I think of a *rut*, I remember my grandfather, who was a farmer and owner of a sawmill. When the huge logging trucks went up the mountain after a heavy rain, they would leave big ruts in the logging road. My grandfather, who had a great sense of humor, placed a sign at the bottom of the mountain which read, "Please choose your rut wisely—You will be in it for 2 miles." If you don't make changes, you may be like thousands of other teachers who have only *survived* life in a rut, but not really *lived life*!

I ask you to make a commitment not only to read these dynamic strategies for success, but to make such a total personal commitment you need to *sign your name*. What is so special about signing your name?

Think about it. Everything significant in your life required a signature. Before you were released from the hospital at birth, someone signed his or her name. When you graduated from high school or college, someone signed his or her name. If you are married, someone signed his or her name. When you made a major purchase or bank loan, you signed your name. Your signature is special because it means you are someone special, and you will do what you agree to do!

IMPORTANT: by signing the *Teacher Success Commitment Pledge* below, you understand that when you *read and apply* the success strategies in this book, you will experience dramatic positive changes in your life— some of them beginning immediately!

## Teacher Success Commitment Pledge

I want to improve my personal and professional life and begin a new journey of success. I want to make my dreams a reality and become the winner in life I was born to be. I realize this requires commitment, change, and honesty with myself. I will read this book in its entirety and complete every exercise and activity. I will apply *all* 6 Dynamic Strategies of Highly Successful Teachers and practice the *10-Day Personal and Professional Power Plan*, knowing with confidence that in doing so. . .

### I WILL BECOME HIGHLY SUCCESSFUL!

_____

Signature

_____

Date

Congratulations on taking the first step out of your comfort zone and committing yourself to the most exciting journey of success you have ever experienced. When you take responsibility for your life and stop blaming others, it is a giant step on your success journey!

I don't know about you, but I enjoy eating good food. I especially like buffets because I can pick and choose all my favorites (which usually include mostly desserts—which I don't need—and very few vegetables—which I really need).

### This book is not an all-you-can-eat-buffet.

In order for these success strategies to work in your life, you cannot choose extra helpings of the ones you like and omit the ones you don't feel comfortable with. Read and do all 6 Dynamic Strategies of Highly Successful Teachers *in the order they are given*, and they will make a profound difference in your personal and professional life!

Reminder: reading and acquiring knowledge about your success will not bring the results in life you desire. *Doing* the right things the right way on a regular basis will help you form positive daily habits. Then you will begin to experience the happy and exciting life you were meant to have! Use your highlighter and pen to complete the Success Activities, mark special thoughts, and write super-special quotes or statements on blank index cards for future reference (the more times you write it, the longer you will remember it). Just Do It!

So, here we go. No excuses accepted—even those signed by your parents. Ever seen that school policy? If you decide to do something and follow through with it, you can accomplish almost anything!

Wherever you are in life, whether just beginning teaching or retiring next month, you must be faithful to your decision to complete the success strategies in this book. Despite the difficult situations you may be experiencing with personal or professional relationships, or heath problems you are facing, you must stick to your commitment.

I want you to get everything out of life you can. . .beginning NOW!

## The Most Important Person in
## Your Success Journey

Success is not a destination, but a journey. All your life you've depended on one person. This person has the ability to determine whether you will wallow in the mire of mediocrity, like thousands of *average* teachers, or begin *right now* to experience a life of excitement and meaningfulness.

That person is you. Not your spouse, children, or friends. Not your students, principal, or school superintendent. . .**YOU!** You are responsible for the direction of your life, either towards sameness or success and significance.

Regardless of what you may have heard, life is not a roll of the dice where some people get lucky and hit the jackpot. We're not talking about winning the lottery. We're talking about developing a plan that will guarantee you *real* success and significance. Ninety-nine percent of the time, people don't make more money and have better personal relationships because they're lucky. They made many choices along the way.

You've also made choices that have resulted in your current status, choices about the college you attended, your friends, your spouse, and even the school where you are employed.

## The Most Important Factor in Your Success Journey

The first and most important step of your success journey is improving the mental picture you have of yourself. Read that statement again. (If you haven't used your highlighter, this would be a great place to start. In fact, take a moment and highlight some of the success principles or quotes you liked up to this point.) Your self-image will determine whether you stay in your *comfort zone* or build the confidence and courage to step out of your *circle of sameness* and begin to experience a new and exciting life.

Many psychologists report that we all lack confidence somewhere in our lives. Often we don't picture ourselves as successful.

As a student, I feared giving an oral book report in front of the class (of course, I would probably have felt more comfortable if I'd actually read the book). As I reflect on this experience, it's interesting that I—the same person who dreaded speaking to 25-30 people—now make my living speaking to hundreds of people, loving every minute of it! The difference? Simply a result of the confidence and belief that resulted from improving my own *self-image*.

I worked at a fast-food restaurant during my college years. As a result of an all-the-food-you-can-eat-policy, I gained about 40 pounds and looked like Humpty Dumpty. When my wife and I got married two years later, I tried every diet imaginable. I dieted religiously—which means I stopped eating while I was in church. I only lost the weight when I began to see myself as a thinner individual, willing to make the necessary changes to keep it off. When my self-image improved, my life, and my waistline, improved.

Teachers often ask, "How can I stay motivated while working with such negative students and peers, and living in such a negative home environment?"

The solution isn't easy, but it is simple:

## All motivation begins with a positive, successful self-image!

You will discover later in this handbook how to motivate others. But it begins with motivating yourself by improving your self-image—the picture of yourself you've painted in your mind.

Changing your self-image really means changing your own mental picture of yourself. Your self-image is revealed in your actions and behavior. You can't hide it.

Your positive self-image is the strong belief you deserve success combined with the belief you can achieve it. Most of the time we tend to focus on the negative aspects of ourselves, which paints a negative self-picture.

For example, what if your principal called you in to his/her office tomorrow and described the great job you're doing but ended the conversation by adding, "There's just one thing I need to mention: your lesson plan book could be a little neater." Would you spend the rest of your day thinking about the principal's positive comments or the constructive criticism at the end of the conversation? Most people agree we tend to think about the negative things more than the positive.

**Focus on the positive!**

List 4 positive things about yourself—two personal and two professional:

1. _____
2. _____
3. _____
4. _____

Improving your self-image and changing your habits go hand-in-hand. Change one and you will automatically change the other. Ninety-five percent of our behavior, our automatic responses and reactions, is based on *habits*. To change your habits, you must have the courage to take different paths. Allow yourself the freedom to make some mistakes. Your journey of success will go much faster when you realize you will learn at least as much from mistakes and failures as your successes.

Answer the following question: Am I excited about the direction I am going in life? If your answer is anything less than enthusiastic, understand that you are meant to enjoy your life NOW—not *after* retirement!

I often hear educators' concerns about improving the self-esteem of students, but how often we omit the importance of improving our own self-esteem by improving our own self-image.

Self-esteem literally means "to appreciate the worth of." When we appreciate the worth of ourselves, we can also appreciate and respect the worth of others. Everyone has something to bring to the table—including you.

**Have patience with all things, but first with yourself. Never confuse your mistakes with your value as a human being. You're a perfectly valuable, creative, worthwhile person simply because you exist. And no amount of triumph or tribulations can ever change that.** *Unconditional self-acceptance* **is the core of a peaceful mind.**

**St. Francis de Sales**

You don't need to impress others. You can enjoy the inner security, without apology, that you're an individual of great worth. Self-worth is quite different from self-conceit. Professional athletes expound, often inappropriately, on their greatness. This is inflated ego, not self-worth. Genuine self-worth comes from feeling comfortable with who you are— *in private as well as in public.*

Our self-worth is also enhanced and encouraged by the encouragement of others. Sadly, however, we often listen to people who negatively impact our self-image. If the significant people in your life cause you to paint a negative self-picture, pursue others who help you to paint a more positive one.

Write the name of one person who has helped you paint a positive portrait of yourself:

_____

Think about how much better this person's encouragement made you feel. Now do the same for others. Your self-image will improve even more if you paint a positive picture for someone else. Make a daily commitment to do *one small act of kindness for someone* without expecting a thank you in return. Beginning today, who will it be?

**Change the "I can'ts" to "I can's"**

Many teachers, like myself, never saw their names on an honor roll. Yet, we sometimes deceive our students by communicating an inaccurate image of our own scholastic success. Honesty with your students is one of the keys to improving your self-image. I know it's not easy, but it's important to be yourself—the *real* you!

Let me summarize my academic merits this way: *I was in the half of my high school graduating class that made the upper half possible!*

Even though I try to put some of my past in a humorous perspective, I maintained a negative self-image from grade school to college. My negative self-image regarding academic potential, combined with the negative reinforcement I received from significant individuals in my life, crippled my performance in school. I really didn't *think* I could do it, so I didn't! A negative self-image in any area of our lives determines our actions and performance.

If you picture yourself as boring and uninteresting, you will remain quiet in group settings. If you convince yourself that you're not athletic, you won't take the risk of getting up to bat.

The most destructive, fixed beliefs don't result from others, but from our own negative self-talk. All of your feelings and emotions results from messages you communicate to yourself! In our internal discourse, we average 45,000 words per day of self-talk, 77% of which is negative and self-defeating.

We allow ourselves to listen to such self-defeating dialogue as:

I can't...do word problems in math, make the team, get a date, get a job, speak to large groups of people, be a funny person, have a positive relationship with my spouse and/or children, do bulletin boards, be a highly successful teacher.

You will learn how to replace your negative self-talk thoughts with more rational, healthy thoughts—instantly—before you finish this chapter!

Remember: when someone makes a negative statement about you, it is simply his or her opinion of you at the moment. You're criticized, perhaps inappropriately, for a mistake. Remember, there is a big difference between *experiencing* a failure and *being* a failure.

> **Failure is an event— not a person.**
> **Yesterday really did end last night.**
> **Today is a brand new day, with new opportunities!**
>
> **Zig Ziglar**

Beginning today, *refuse to allow someone else to label you.* And don't use negative self-talk to put the label on yourself. Most often, labels are just dressed up excuses for not doing something worthwhile in our life. Labels are endless, such as, I'm too. . .poor, short, tall, fat, skinny, spastic, stupid, ugly, quiet. . .The list is endless. Don't make excuses! You can do things you thought you never thought possible when you drop the labels and excuses. You can be successful. Believe it! Every day remind yourself:

### Who I see is who I'll be!

A teacher once shared his story with me of how he was labeled "Most Likely to Fail" as a senior in high school. Although no more than an inappropriate joke played by the yearbook staff, he embraced the label and spent the next 20 years in failed relationships and numerous jobs. Only recently had he understood the powerful principle of rejecting negative and inaccurate portraits.

Our actions are consistent with our self-image. A teacher will lack control in class if he or she paints an insecure self-portrait. You must see yourself in control of that hard-to-control student or class.

A teacher who lacks rapport and connection with his students will prove this picture to be correct by his behavior— rarely joking and not volunteering for clubs or activities that encourage student interaction. His actions back up the picture. And guess what? He is exactly right. *Who he sees is who he'll be.*

A recent study concluded that happy people were much more likely to involve themselves in others' lives. Low self-esteem, resulting in a poor self-image, acts as a roadblock on the journey of success. We allow a poor self-image to inhibit us from involving ourselves with the *right* people. Many people with a poor self-image are involved with others, but the *others* are most often negative, sarcastic gripers who just want them to join the club. To improve your success potential, associate with people who possess a success mentality and share your goal of wanting the most out of life!

**Change the mental picture of yourself and you will
change your behavior.**

**Change your behavior and you will
experience success!**

Picture yourself as the person you would like to become and begin acting as *that person.* Eventually, *who you see is who you'll be!*

At home, a teacher may picture himself as an inadequate spouse or parent. If so, even an insignificant mistake will further convince you that your picture is true. Your portrait is the foundation of your entire personality, and behavior. It even helps determine the circumstances you remain in. They're all built on your self-image.

Write two sentences describing your current self-portrait. Not the picture you want to paint— your current painting. Include both the good and bad aspects of this picture.

Now write two more sentences and identify those negative details. How many are real, and how many are just "talk?"

> **What your mind can conceive, and your heart can believe, YOU CAN ACHIEVE!**
>
> **William James**

The great news is **YOU CAN CHANGE**! But you must believe you can change every concern and challenge you listed above into a positive strength. The key is to change your beliefs about yourself.

### If it is to be. . .it is up to me!

The results of making the effort to improve? Teachers, once considering early retirement, now look forward to Monday morning at school. Why? Their circumstances haven't changed—they've changed!

You'll need imagination to form new pictures of yourself. Do you remember your Kindergarten teacher posing the deep and philosophical question: "What would you like to be when you grow up?" Your imagination immediately transported you to a place only royalty, saints, and heroes are allowed. Felt real, didn't it?

Humans react to their *perception* of the truth. <u>Your nervous system cannot distinguish the difference between an imagined or a real experience</u>. People who are hypnotized are told to imagine their hand is hot. Tests have proven their skin temperature actually rises and in many cases a blister will actually form. All because they *imagine* they feel hot.

Professional basketball players pause before they shoot every free throw to visualize (imagine) the ball going through the hoop. Their brain informs them that the shot is successful. Again, your mind doesn't know the difference between reality and what is imagined.

Teachers can utilize visualization in the same way. Imagine the behavior of specific challenging students. Now visualize yourself with control in a difficult situation involving those students. Be specific in your imagination: what you will say, your facial expression, etc. Use this exercise every day and eventually your picture of controlling the situation will become a reality.

You must also *expect* your desired outcome to occur. Have high expectations of yourself and don't let negative people convince you otherwise. Sometimes this requires drastic action. Do whatever is necessary to make a positive change.

One teacher shared with me that everyone at the faculty lunch table griped from the moment they sat down until they finished eating. Her mood soured in her afternoon classes, and she didn't finish her work. She took action. She decided to keep in touch with her peers, but decided to do it individually and at another time. From then on she brought her lunch and ate in her classroom.

Understand, I'm not suggesting you follow this teacher's example. Social fellowship with your colleagues is very important to teamwork. I *am* suggesting you consider the input you allow into your mind, positive or negative— and where it originates. Realize you'll act on the picture painted of yourself and others.

Again, a healthy self-image is based on positive *self-worth*. You are worth more than you can imagine because you were created in God's image and, as one first grader told her teacher: "God don't make no junk." In fact, it is an insult to our Creator to say we are unimportant and unworthy or incapable of accomplishing great things in life. He doesn't create failures, and He is responsible for creating you!

## Important Self-Image Principles

<u>Instructions:</u> Write these principles on index cards. Choose a different card each day. Carry it with you and quickly glance at it every opportunity you have. As busy as you are, you will be surprised how

many times you will be able to read your thought-for-the-day. You will still have those "bummer" days, but it is amazing how the number of great days will increase by doing this. So what do you have to lose? Nothing. Try it. It works!

1. I have unique talents and abilities. I will accept and appreciate the ways I am different from others.

2. I will not compare myself to others. No one is perfect.

3. I understand what others say to me or about me is only their *opinion* and *not reality*.

4. I have the power to make choices than can change my personal and professional life by changing the picture/self-image of myself.

5. I will forgive myself for past mistakes and stop mentally beating myself up. I will also release all blame and resentment for wrongs done to me. I will forgive others for their mistakes.

6. I will stop making excuses and take control of my choices in the classroom and at home.

7. I understand no one owes my anything, because it is a debt that I will never collect. I will not let others control my happiness and success.

8. I won't take criticism personally and I'll look for the *right* in my students, peers, family and friends - instead of the wrongs or how I have been slighted.

9. I will begin a personal wellness program. My health is important to me.

10. I will dress-up at least one time a week— because I know the better I look, the better I will feel about myself.

11. I will look for something humorous that happens in my classroom and share it with someone every day.

Laughter is the first sign of a positive self-image, especially the ability to laugh at myself *when* I make mistakes. Did you watch the comedy *What About Bob?* Bob's psychiatrist told him he must take "baby-steps" on his way to recovery. Don't expect your world to change overnight. Be willing to do the little things that make a big difference. Do more than read and underline or highlight important success principles in this book. *Experience* them by using a proven plan of action.

At the end of each chapter, you'll be given a specific plan of action to implement immediately. These are the baby-steps that will lead to your 10-Day Personal Power Plan of Action at the end of the book.

## Strategy #1
## PLAN OF ACTION

What is Teacher Success Strategy #1? (The title of Chapter One.)

_____

_____


List 6 successes you have already experienced. Three of these should be personal (such as— been married x number of years, being a good cook, etc.), and 3 should be professional (such as—graduated from college majoring in education, head of a school committee, etc.)

_____

_____

_____

_____

_____

_____

List 4 important qualities you offer people in your life; for example, patience, empathy, etc.

_____

_____

_____

_____

List 4 people, or groups of people, you care about.

_____        _____

_____        _____

Write two humorous things that happened in the past 2-3 days, at home or school.

_____        _____

Read *My Personal Commitment Promise* out loud, every day before you leave home and before you go to bed in the evening. Place a check on your cards each time you repeat the promise. Leave one card in a convenient place in your bedroom or kitchen and one on your class-room desk or work area. The more often you read these qualities, the more quickly they will become a reality for you. Read all of them every day and they will become the truth.

### 1<sup>st</sup> Week

| | | |
|---|---|---|
| Monday | __ a.m. | __ p.m. |
| Tuesday | __ a.m. | __ p.m. |
| Wednesday | __ a.m. | __ p.m. |
| Thursday | __ a.m. | __ p.m. |
| Friday | __ a.m. | __ p.m. |
| Saturday | __ a.m. | __ p.m. |
| Sunday | __ a.m. | __ p.m. |

**My Personal Commitment Promise**

I, _____, am an honest, intelligent, optimistic person who is enthusiastic about my possibilities in life! I am a hardworking teacher who is energetic and a team player with members of my faculty, students, and family. I am teachable and want to learn every day how to be the winner I was meant to be! My family and friends are important to me and I will make special time for them every day. I am motivated to do my best so that my healthy self-image will remain on solid ground. These are the qualities, which enable me to be the right kind of person, to do the right things, to have more success tomorrow than today! **I AM COMMITTED TO MAKING IT HAPPEN!**

The significance of improving our self-image and thinking the right thoughts for success relate closely to each other, but are two separate strategies for a reason. We must know our self-worth and value (Chapter One), before we change our thinking and establish a positive mind-set for success (Chapter Two). All the positive thinking in the world won't improve your life if you don't first *Unleash Your Personal Power With a Dynamic Self-Image!*

Now that you have taken that first big step on your journey of success, *are you excited about changing your thinking so that you can change your life?* You have to think it to make it happen! Continue painting a positive self-portrait and get ready for the second Strategy for Highly Successful Teachers. . .

# SUCCESS

To laugh often and love much; to win the respect of intelligent persons and the affection of children; to earn the approbation of honest critics and endure the betrayal of false friends; to appreciate beauty; to find the best in others; to give of one's self; to leave the world a bit better, whether by a healthy child, a garden patch or a redeemed social condition; to have played and laughed with enthusiasm and sung with exultation; to know even one life has breathed easier because you have lived. This is to have succeeded!

Ralph Waldo Emerson

"I am aware of people's feelings and I sense you are experiencing a great deal of stress in your life. . .would you like to talk about it?

*by Chris King*

# "Success Notes & Quotes"

"I don't mind that my son is making more money than I did
my first year of teaching. What bothers me is he is only six years old
and it's his allowance!"

# Teacher Success Strategy 2

## CHANGE YOUR THOUGHTS AND
## YOU CAN CHANGE YOUR LIFE!

A few years ago some teacher colleagues and I sat down at the opening session of an educators' conference, just as the keynote speaker wound up.

"If you will just *think* positive thoughts, you can do *anything* you want to do!" he exclaimed—as he jumped two feet up from the stage. He continued, "There isn't anything you cannot do if you put your mind to it and think positively. Anything is possible if you just think positive thoughts."

Let's see, he said if I just think positive thoughts, I can do anything. So when I get home I'll take my two sons, Jon and Chris, to the school gym. Then I'll think positive thoughts about performing a helicopter slam dunk, starting my "ups" at the foul line. All I have to do is think positively, right?

You get my point. But don't toss out the baby with the bath water. Our speaker only told part of the story. In addition to developing a healthy self-image, as you discovered in "Teaching Strategy #1," you increase your opportunity for success by changing the way you think.

**"My heart is singing for joy this morning. A miracle has happened! The light of understanding has shone upon my little pupil's mind, and behold, all things have changed!"**

**Annie Sullivan, American teacher of the deaf**

**"I was only a little mass of possibilities. It was my teacher (Annie Sullivan) who unfolded and developed them. . .She never since let pass an opportunity. . .to make my life sweet and useful."**

**Helen Keller, American writer**

## Two Important Factors of Changing for Success

1. Realize that the power of your thoughts and beliefs determines who you are and who you can become!

2. Believe you CAN change your life by changing the attitudes of your mind!

**"The biggest discovery in our generation is that human beings, by changing the inner attitudes of their minds, can change the outer aspects of their lives!"**

**William James, Psychologist**
**Harvard University**

*Everything you are up to at this point in your life, and everything you will become, is the sum total of your thoughts.* (Don't miss this powerful success principle—read it again.)

Do you want to improve the quality of your personal and professional life? Then improve the quality of your thoughts.

You are probably familiar with Special Olympics, the outstanding organization involved with helping people experience success. One of their brochures states. . . **"It's ALL About Attitude!"**

Think about how powerful that statement is! When you consider any area of your life - physical, mental, spiritual, financial, etc.— **how successful you will be is completely determined by your attitude.**

## ATTITUDE

*The longer I live, the more I realize the impact of attitude on my life. In my opinion, attitude is more important than facts. It is more important than the past, than education, than money, than circumstances, than failures, than successes, than what other people think or say or do. It is more important than appearance, giftedness, or skill. It will make or break a company. . .a church. . .a home.*

*The remarkable thing is **we have a choice every day** regarding the attitude we will embrace for that day. We cannot change our past...we cannot change the fact that people will act in a certain way.*

*We cannot change the inevitable. The only thing we can do is play on the one string we have, and that is our attitude.*

*I am convinced that life is **10% what happens to me and 90% how I react to it**. And so it is with you. **We may not be in charge of our circumstances, but we <u>are</u> in charge of our attitudes!***

Reread the phrases in bold type. Your attitude is *your* choice, and your choice will determine your future.

"Now wait a minute, Jerry," you may be thinking. "You're telling me that I chose my family problems? If I had known my spouse was a good-for-nothing loser, I would have never gotten married."

"And what about the terrible class my principal gave me this year? I thought last year's class was bad, but this is *definitely* the worst group of kids I've ever had in my umpteen years of teaching! Believe me, if I had a *choice*, I wouldn't be teaching this class!"

"What about my health problems? You think I have a *choice* about this nagging lower-back-pain I feel every time I walk around the class?"

Whew! Take a big breath, come back to earth, and listen to the context of "choice"— in relation to your success in life. But let's blast before we build. Choice doesn't mean that you always have a choice. You may not be able to choose your health, your family situations, or your students. (We *do*, however, have more choices than we realize and sometimes want to admit).

---

**I refuse to lose!**

---

**Answer this question concerning choice:**

*Do you think there is something you can specifically do in the next ten days that would make your personal and professional life better?*

By saying yes to that question you're saying that **regardless of what has happened in the past or is happening now in your life, you believe there are things you can do right now that can change your future. The choice is yours!**

**Please rewrite the following statement:**

*"My future at home and at school depends on the choices I make about situations and people. I will make the changes necessary to become the winner in life I was created to be!"*

Complaining and griping can also affect our attitude and inhibit our changes for success.

**Remember, one bad apple can spoil the whole basket.** Complainers enjoy dragging you into the dark regions of their negativity just like a vacuum. Ever notice how one teacher can make a negative comment to several teachers about something and within seconds the entire group has jumped on the "complaining bandwagon?" It's like dominos— you push one and they all fall down.

**Caution:** on a scale of 1-10, where do *you* rate on the "complaint scale?" Complaining is easy to do. In fact, it can be downright ·fun sometimes, especially if we laugh while doing it. It seems so harmless.

However, complaining on a regular basis can be dangerous to your attitude and thought patterns for success. Ever known a negative person, someone who complains, yet retains the respect of fellow teachers and students? Of course not, because they don't exist.

Why? Teachers can't possibly be positive and enthusiastic about making a difference in students' lives while at the same time constantly griping. The two simply don't go together.

☑ **Please place a checkmark beside the items you have complained about during the past week:**

| | |
|---|---|
| _____ Weather | _____ Teacher's Responsibilities |
| _____ Family/Friends | _____ School Meetings |
| _____ Home Responsibilities | _____ Student's Parents |
| _____ Teachers' Salaries/Benefits | _____ School Administrators |

There's a difference in venting our emotions and in constantly complaining.

## Success Strategy for Decreasing Complaints

Choose two blank index cards from your pack. At the top of one of the index cards write the words **Complaint Card**. At the top of the other index card, write the words **Compliment Card**. Take note of your complaints and compliments by writing a tally-mark on the appropriate card when you say either one. Through this exercise you'll learn to "think before you speak." Soon you'll be able to proactively gauge the impact (positive or negative) of what you are going to say.

Keep a record of your complaints and compliments for 5 days and you will find yourself: in a better mood, more upbeat and energetic, getting more things done, and more fun for others to be around –at school and at home.

I've observed teachers experiencing results so dramatic they could hardly believe it themselves. One teacher said he actually went through an entire day without spouting a complaint. He said it was his best day of teaching in over ten years!

Another teacher told me of an idea she devised to combat the negative nature of her fellow faculty members. Every complaint uttered resulted in a fifty cent contribution to what her department affectionately called the "Gotcha Jar." At the end of the month, her department used the proceeds to purchase breakfast. Great idea, and great fun.

You may be thinking, "With all the complaining I hear from the teachers on our faculty, after only one week of using the "Gotcha Jar," we would probably have enough money to send everyone on a seven day cruise to the Bahamas!" Sounds like a better idea every time I hear it.

---

**"Don't let the things you can't do, interfere with the things you can do!"**

**John Wooden**

---

In addition to the *Chronic Complainer*, another easily identifiable negative person is the _Badmouth Blamer_. Did you know the first record of blame occurred in the Bible?

God told Adam and Eve, "Enjoy life, but don't eat anything from the tree in the middle of the garden." Of course, just like your students, they did exactly what they were not supposed to do.

One evening God was hiking through the garden and asked Adam why he ate the fruit. Adam replied, "Well, you know that woman, Eve? She made me do it." As Zig Ziglar says when explaining this story, "We all know the real problem wasn't the apple in the tree, but the 'pair' on the ground."

Blame and justify. Blame and justify. When we blame others, as Adam did, we shirk responsibility. **Successful people begin by accepting responsibility for their situation and then starting an action plan to deal with it.** They refuse to blame people for their situation.

**It's not where you start that matters, it's where you finish!**

Some teachers **"If"** themselves to death. We all have our favorites. What are some of yours?

**"If** I had a better spouse. . ."

**"If** I had a better principal. . ."

**"If** I had better students. . ."

**"If** I had more supportive parents. . ."

**"If** I made more money. . ."

**"If. . .If. . .If. . ."**

Blaming our lack of success in any area of our life on these or other factors is a cop-out to facing the situation and making a decision to do something about it.

Before my mother passed away, after a courageous five-year fight with cancer, she gave a soul-searching talk to many church groups titled, *"Bloom Where You Are Planted."* She shared how everyone faces challenges in life, but how we overcome these challenges, *instead of blaming others* (especially people who had nothing to do with our situation), is the sign of a person who will accomplish great things in life.

*Blaming or complaining has never made people or situations improve.* In fact, they have more of a negative effect on our daily performance than you can imagine. Both dramatically affect our *thinking*— and *that* is exactly what Teacher Success Strategy #2 is about.

Discover for yourself why *how we think* is so important. The September 15, 2000 issue of *Investor's Business Daily* featured the following list of the traits successful people—including teachers - possess. Traits that **can turn your dreams into reality.** (Trait number one is described in this chapter and traits number two and three are described in the next chapter.)

## Secrets to Success

1.  **How you *think* is EVERYTHING!** Always be positive. Think success, not failure. Be aware of a negative environment.

2.  **Decide upon your true dreams and goals.** *Write down* your specific goals and develop a plan to reach them.

3.  **Take action.** Goals are nothing without action. Get started now. Just do it.

Get your *highlighter ready because* **you are about to discover the super-charged principles of how the thoughts in your mind decide your degree of success in life!**

> **Negative input (information) never results in positive output (behavior).**

**You choose and change your thoughts and behavior by choosing and changing the information you feed your mind! Consistently change the information you are listening to, reading and watching, and your behavior will change! Is that exciting or what?!!**

Following are seven sources of information used to feed your mind. Please place a check under one of the columns indicating whether you think the information from that source is *More Negative or More Positive.*

|  | SOURCE | |
| --- | :---: | :---: |
|  | **More Positive** | **More Negative** |
| 1. Television | _____ | _____ |
| 2. Newspaper | _____ | _____ |
| 3. Books | _____ | _____ |
| 4. Radio | _____ | _____ |
| 5. Other People's Conversation | _____ | _____ |
| 6. Your own Self-Talk | _____ | _____ |
| 7. Computer | _____ | _____ |
| 8. Other: _____ | _____ | _____ |

If you watched the 6:30 evening news lately, out of approximately 24 stories, how many do you think focus on the positive aspects of life? If you guessed 1-3, you are correct. During a typical day of school, do you think your mind hears more compliments and motivational information from other teacher, students, and administrators—or do you hear more complaining, blaming, and criticizing? Remember— only positive input can produce positive output.

Highly successful teachers *choose* (there's that word again—*choose*) to focus on the positive input in their minds to replace the negative.

We know **it takes twelve positive statements to replace one negative statement.** We have a challenge every day to focus on the positive, but it's an exciting challenge. This is the difference between highly successful teachers and teachers who finish their careers in apathetic, ho-hum mediocrity.

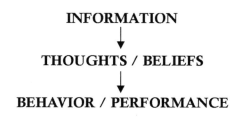

**INFORMATION**
↓
**THOUGHTS / BELIEFS**
↓
**BEHAVIOR / PERFORMANCE**

**Choose to change the information you put in your mind and your thoughts, beliefs, and behavior will change!**
**(Change your input and you will change your output).**

Have you ever done something so many times, you did it without even thinking about it?

This is a phenomenal function of our success-thinking process accomplished by using our **subconscious mind.** We use our **conscious mind** when we are aware of what we are doing. But by doing something repetitiously, our subconscious mind is programmed to do it without consciously thinking, "I am doing this."

What does this have to do with being an effective teacher?

**Your subconscious mind is a key to you becoming and remaining a highly successful teacher!** Why? Because by following the action plan you are about to learn, you can reprogram your mind to eliminate the negative programming.

## Two Simple Steps for Changing to Success Thinking: Stop and Start!

<u>**STOP!**</u> Stop complaining and griping about people or situations beyond your control.

Stop— as much negative information as possible from entering your mind.

Stop— listening to or watching the news, or reading it in the newspaper to start or end your day!

<u>**START**</u>: Start listening to a positive tape or read something positive for the first 10 minutes and the last 10 minutes of your day!

Personally, I listen while I am shaving each morning. Female teachers tell me they use it while they are putting on their makeup. I realized if I am going to "just stand there" a few minutes every day, that's valuable time I could use to put positive information in my mind, without taking up any "extra" time.

How many consecutive meals have you missed in your life? What would happen to you if you didn't eat physical food for several days? Loss of energy, headaches, and the loss of your ability to function properly are among the many ways you would be affected. The same is true with the necessity of a daily positive mental diet! You cannot wait until you are stressed, frustrated, and depressed to begin your positive diet. **Your mind must be fed success thoughts <u>every</u> <u>day</u>,** so you will be able to overcome the challenges at school and at home you will face— <u>every</u> <u>day</u>!

> **Motivation is like taking a bath. . .You can't do it just
> one time and
> expect it to last forever!**

## Success Suggestion No. 2:
## Use positive self-talk affirmation cards.

One teacher shared how he was surrounded by faculty members who were constantly negative. He carried his PAC (Positive Affirmation Card) with him all day, to use as *ammunition* against negative comments and thoughts. When people would start griping and complaining, he would quietly and quickly, without anyone noticing, glance at his PAC for a morale boost for the negative situation.

Follow this action plan for fifteen days and you will begin to see a different person when you look in the mirror! Your gray hair—or no hair—condition may still exist, but it won't matter as much because **you will begin to change and improve where it matters most...from inside your mind and heart!**

## Key Success Principles
## of Strategy #2

1. Improving your quality of life is truly *ALL about attitude!*

2. You have a *choice* of what you will do with your situation in life!

3. *Stop* complaining and blaming!

4. *Start* reprogramming your subconscious (success) mind by using Positive Affirmation Cards, listening to positive tapes, and reading motivational literature.

## Success Strategy #2
## PLAN OF ACTION

Write Success Strategy #1:

_____

Write Success Strategy #2:

_____

List two specific things you will *stop complaining* about— <u>beginning today</u>.

_____

_____

What success training tape will you listen to first? (Your favorite, or refer to the resource list on page 128.):

_____

If you do not have a supply of index cards (to use for Positive Affirmation Cards), when and where will you purchase them?

_____

Name two people you find it difficult to communicate with in a positive manner. Make a commitment to smile and ask them how they are doing.

_____      _____

**WOW!** You are making great progress on your new journey of success! You are forming a more positive mental picture of yourself—self-image—and are working on a personal plan of action to change our thinking from failure to success!

While continuing to be a winner in the areas of self-image and positive thinking, you are now preparing to take the third step of improving your personal and professional life by learning how to manage stress and teacher burnout. Success Strategy #3—**Strangle Stress and Extinguish the Fires of Teacher Burnout**—will help you learn how to be successful, even when you have "one of those days, or weeks, or months, or. . ."

At this point, you know I expect you to make a positive affirmation that you are ready for the next dynamic strategy to become a highly successful teacher. Managing stress is the next important step on your journey of personal and professional success. Are you ready? Please answer enthusiastically, **"YES— I am ready!!"**

> "Teaching kids how to count is fine, but teaching them what counts is best."
>
> Bob Talbert

# Teacher Success Strategy 3

## STRANGLE STRESS AND EXTINGUISH THE FIRES OF TEACHER BURNOUT!

"I've *had it!*" you say to yourself.

- I've *had it* up to *here* with all the papers to grade!
- I've *had it* with all the meetings!
- I've *had it* with all the extra "duties!"
- I've *had it* with discipline problems!
- I've *had it* with state mandated tests!
- I've *had it* with low pay!
- I've *had it* with unsupportive administrative and parents!

And I have *definitely* had it with rude, obnoxious, apathetic students, who don't really care whether they do well in school or not! "I used to actually enjoy teaching," you've probably said at one time or another, "but it's just not worth it anymore. First chance I get. . .I'm 'outta here!"

It wouldn't be quite as serious if teachers contemplated these thoughts at the *end* of one of "those days" and only once in awhile. But many teachers find themselves in this mind-set before they leave home or on the way to school— on a regular basis.

**To make matters worse, you finally arrive at school and. . .**

You're late for bus duty because you couldn't find your car keys or matching shoes. Taking the shortcut to school at 85 mph, you noticed the gas tank was below empty. Somehow, you "landed" in the parking lot on fumes, and as you run to the cafeteria, two students are fighting on the floor as your principal stands in the door looking at her watch, as if to say, "You <u>do</u> know this is going in your permanent performance file, right?"

After taking roll at the beginning of your first class, the assistant principal walks in and informs you he will be observing you during the next hour. He asks to review your lesson plans for the day. For five minutes you frantically and unsuccessfully search for them when suddenly it hits you. . .they are at home on the kitchen table!

About 10 minutes into the observation, one student boldly asks, "Why are we doing all this written work so early? You usually give us *free time* and we don't <u>ever</u> do anything for at least 20-30 minutes." (You look for a hole in the floor to drop through. There isn't one.)

Your assistant principal immediately begins writing and fills at least 3 pages in his yellow legal pad— which you <u>know</u> is not a good sign. Even though the rest of your classes proceed in similar fashion, you push on and make it to the final bell. The bell rings just as the last student leaves your classroom. At that moment the principal says those magic words on the PA system, "All teachers are reminded of the extended faculty meeting this afternoon in the library. We have some very important things to discuss so be prepared for the meeting to last until at least 6:00 p.m."

Somehow you endure 2½ hours on such "important" topics as whether to serve Coke or Pepsi at the next parent open-house, and who would like to serve on the committee for the special community program to be held year after next.

As you finally pull in the driveway, your entire family is waiting on the front porch and you realize this is Family Night Out for Pizza.

You drag yourself and your forty-five pound book-bag out of the car as one of them yells, "Why are you late? You only work until 3:30. It seems like you could at least respect our plans enough to get home on time!"

You fall on your knees in the yard and sob uncontrollably as you hear someone ask, "What did I say? All I asked was why were you late?"

They leave for pizza without you. It's the only <u>good thing</u> that's happened all day!!

Hopefully, you don't have too many days like this. But odds are if you've taught for at least one week, you have experienced days when you were so stressed out you wondered whether teaching was worth all the hassles.

What do you *really* know about stress— other than you are fairly certain you experience it frequently? All stress is not bad. *Eustress* is the kind of euphoric sensation experienced when your favorite team is trying to win in the final seconds of the game. Just like the athletes, your adrenaline is flowing and you're excited. You experience nervousness and stress, but it affects you positively. In fact, just like the athletes, it is possible to perform better when you experience eustress. You probably experienced eustress your first day of teaching.

*Distress* is the kind of unpleasant and/or harmful sensation experienced when faced with *too much to do and not enough time to do it*. For example, *distress* occurs at the end of a grading period when you are trying to complete your report cards. The pressure is on and you're not a happy camper. Since teachers seem to experience more *distress* than *eustress* at school, Teacher Success Strategy #3, **Strangle**

**Stress and Extinguish the Fires of Teacher Burnout,** will help you manage your negative distress levels at home and school. Remember: stress at home *does* affect your performance in the classroom.

One of my goals for this book is to help you experience a life of happiness and fulfillment with less worries, doubt and, stress—a life that will help you reach more of your potential as a person and a teacher.

Don't wait for retirement to start enjoying life. You can enjoy your career as a teacher—starting now! But you must understand the effects of stress on your life. Unmanaged stress can dramatically affect you at school and at home.

The way to control stress can literally be a matter of life and death. Here are some of the facts about stress revealed through medical research:

- Stress is the number one factor in heart disease!
- 95% of all tension headaches are caused by stress!
- 90% of all teachers say they experience stress at least 2-4 times per week!
- Stress has passed the common cold as the most prevalent health problem in the U.S.!
- Stress contributed to 8 of the top 10 causes of death among Americans!
- 65% of patient visits to family practice physicians or internists have nothing to do with medical diseases. The symptoms are real, but the cause of the symptoms is *stress*!

In my experience, I've found that the personal toll of stress on teachers is dramatic! In addition to its affect on your health, unmanaged stress can result in: absenteeism, inadequate time spent preparing lessons, less patience assisting students who need additional one-on-one help, and strained family/personal relationships.

Before we see where we are going, we must first know where we are. Completing the *Teacher Stress Self-Assessment* is a great starting point to focus on your specific area of concern.

**Please complete the following Teacher Stress Self-Assessment. Write the letter of your choice to indicate how often, during the past year, these situations created stress for you.**

**Key: N = Never, S = Sometimes, O = Often**

## Teacher Stress Self-Assessment

Personal Stress:

N 1. Your own health or the health of family or friends
N 2. Marriage or relationships with others
S 3. Moving out of a place of residence
S 4. Your household/family responsibilities
N 5. Vacation
N 6. Lack of time spent with family or friends
S 7. Lack of leisure-time for yourself
N 8. Death of someone close to you

Job-Related Stress:

S 9. My job as a teacher is demanding and creates tension.
S 10. I feel tired and not physically ready for work.
S 11. My schedule or teacher responsibilities create problems.
S 12. I experience conflict with students, other educators and parents.
N 13. I changed teaching jobs or major responsibilities (one time = "S").
N 14. I miss work because I need a mental break or have personal problems.
N 15. Generally speaking, I feel my job is boring and unchallenging.
S 16. Generally speaking, I feel the morale at our school should be better.

N___ 17. Generally speaking, I don't see very much hu-
mor/laughter in my life.

**Total Number of S's:___ Total Number of O's:___**

If your total number of "S's" and "O's" (when added together)
exceeds 8, you could be in the danger zone and need to take the action steps given in this chapter to manage stress and take better control of your life.

### "Teacher Stress is. . ."

- Losing your grade book 2 days before report cards are due.
- Remembering you left the class pet at school over spring break.
- Teaching a computer class to students who know more about computers than you do.
- Setting your alarm clock on "p.m." instead of "a.m." the first day of school.
- Your worst student returning to your classroom as a student-teacher.
- Having the superintendent's or school board chairperson's child in your class.
- When a student wants to know if his parent's lawsuit against the school district will affect his grade.
- Having to borrow lunch money from your students.
- Grading a complete set of tests— using the wrong answer key.
- When the school nurse shows up at your classroom to per-form a head lice check.
- Leading the committee for textbook selection.

- After counting students on a school field trip, coming up one short.
- Finding out your students' best achievement test scores are the lowest in the school.
- Hearing one of your "discipline-challenging students" say, "My dad wants a conference with you tomorrow morning and he is *really* mad!"

(*Erasing My Insanity*, Kimberly Chambers)

When I drive my car and the gas gauge on the dashboard starts flashing "Low Fuel," it is a warning signal to me that if I don't refill the tank soon, I will be thumbing a ride to the nearest service station. Just as the gasoline gauge signals a warning regarding the fuel level in my car, our body gives us warning signals to slow down and refuel. If we don't heed the warning signals, we will pay the consequences listed earlier.

> **"We might cease thinking of school as a place, and learn to believe that it is basically relationships between children and adults, and between children and children."**
>
> **George Dennison**

Some of the warning signals our body gives us include: increased tension headaches, loss of energy and enthusiasm, impatience, quick temper, rapid pulse, insomnia, fatigue, and loss of appetite. Have any of these warning lights been flashing in your life lately? Refer to the *Teacher Stress Self-Assessment* and circle the number beside each statement you marked as "O" = Often. Focus on these specific areas during Teacher Success Strategy #3.

**Our *perspective* of circumstances— not the circumstance itself— determines our stress level.** Our perspective - how we "see" things— results in endless, energy-draining *worry* about a circumstance. **Psychologists report that 80% of our "worry list" shouldn't exist for two reasons:**

1. We can't to anything about the situation.

2. The circumstance we fear hasn't even occurred yet.

Personally, I've wasted a lot of good brain cells with worry, building a mountain range out of molehills. Imagine for a moment you are the parent of a teenager who is completing the first semester of college. (Maybe you are like me and don't have to *imagine*— those tuition bills are for real!) Throughout the fall you assume all is well until one day during the first week of December, you receive the following letter in the mail:

*Dear Mom and Dad:*

*Please sit down before you read this letter. (You already <u>know</u> this isn't going to be good news, right?) I'm doing okay now, since the dormitory fire, thanks to the loving care of our custodian, Norman. Since that incredible night in September, I've spent almost every waking hour with Norman, and he has helped me get to know my real self. You see, he didn't just pull me from the fire— he became my entire life!*

*Yes, we're living together now and I know you will learn to love him as deeply as I do. Oh yes, one more thing— I'm pregnant and starting to show. I know how thrilled you must be, considering how much you always wanted to be a grandparent.*

*Your loving daughter,*

*Mary*

*P.S. There was no fire. I'm not pregnant and, in fact, there is no Norman. However, this semester I <u>am</u> going to flunk Biology and just wanted you to put it in the proper perspective!*

What if you received a letter like that? Would you "keep your cool" or have a "heebie-jeebie fit" in the middle of the floor?

Dr. Richard Carlson, in his series of books, *"Don't Sweat the Small: It's All Small Stuff,"* tells us to **"Stop living in the emergency zone!"** In other words, everything that happens in your life that's not planned is not a national emergency. Learn to *go with the flow.*

During my first year of teaching I met a teacher whose life was so structured he would literally "lose it" when we had a fire drill. As the students said to him, "Mr. Franklin, get a life!" Like Mr. Franklin, many people fail to recognize the causes or *Triggers of Stress.*

## Stress Triggers

### At School:

1. **Recent Events** such as major *changes* in policies or procedures, mandatory increase in work hours, sudden significant increases in the activity level or pace of work, major reorganization.

2.  **Ongoing Conditions** at school such as too much work to do in too little time, feedback only when performance is unsatisfactory, temperature in your classroom, noise, interruptions, meetings after school hours, deadlines, conflicts between you and students or coworkers, unclear standards and expectations, etc.

## Away from School:

1.  **Recent Ev**ents such as marriage, death of someone close, illness— as well as restriction of your social life to the point where you don't have enough time for friends and family, hobbies, etc.

2.  **Ongoing Conditions** such as personal finances/bills, anxiety and worry about your children's activities, your career plans, etc.

Each of the *Stress Triggers* can throw us into a mental state of anxiety and *frustration*. So, what can you do to handle frustrations?

**F**ace the issue and find a resolution.

**R**efuse to leave until the task is completed.

**U**nderstand the fears you attached to the event.

**S**top procrastinating and begin right now.

**T**ake it at a manageable pace. Slow down and walk, not run.

**R**efuse to walk away until you have solved the problem.

**A**sk for help if you can't get it done on your own. Sometimes we need a professional counselor. Sometimes we just need a close friend.

**T**ruth is critical. Most people aren't honest about their emotions and frustrations.

**I**nternal discipline is a must. Many people talk themselves out of finishing.

**O**pen yourself to challenge on your position.

**N**ever procrastinate. I repeat. . .**Never procrastinate**!

Believe it or not, there **is** a positive side of stress. . .

### "Stressed, spelled backwards is. . .Desserts!"

The person responsible for the condition of your self-image also determines the perspective you keep on stress. Understanding how to manage stress is part of understanding yourself. Have you ever done something and later thought, "Why did I act that way?"

The better you understand yourself, the better you can manage stress as well as your relationships to students, colleagues, family and friends. The DISC Profile is one of the most effective tools to determine how to understand yourself as well as how you currently manage stress. This self-assessment has been used by schools, Fortune 500 companies, and leading organizations for over 20 years in over 35 countries! Understanding my DISC Profile has helped me deal with the frustrations and stress of life and successfully relate to people different from me.

## Different Strokes for Different Folks

The purpose of the DISC is not to force you into a profiled "box," but to help identify your blend of characteristics and traits that enable you to function as a unique and valuable individual.

We all have one to two dominant characteristics, but everyone is a unique combination of all 4 categories of DISC. (You are not either a D or I or S or C, but a blend of each). I can't wait for you to see yourself in the DISC. Look - and you will find YOU!

## DISC Profile of Behavior Tendencies

Do you consider yourself generally to be:

1.  *Fast-Paced*— outgoing, taking risk, taking action, enjoying talking/telling, or

2.  *Slow-Paced*— reflective, reserved, avoiding risk, thinking carefully through decisions

Do you consider yourself generally to be:

1.  *People Oriented*— sharing opinions and feelings, considering relationships a high priority, or

2.  *Task Oriented*— planning your work, considering facts/data for decisions

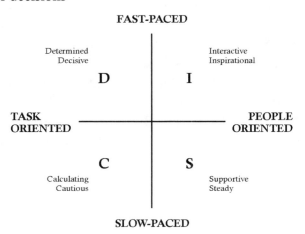

FAST-PACED

| Determined Decisive | | Interactive Inspirational |

D     I

TASK ORIENTED         PEOPLE ORIENTED

C     S

| Calculating Cautious | | Supportive Steady |

SLOW-PACED

You've probably already identified whether you are people oriented or task oriented. *After reading the description of behavior tendencies below, write a number beside each of them, according to which best describes you, most of the time. (#1=the tendency that describes you most; #4=the tendency that describes you least.)* For example, after reading all the descriptions, if you feel the "I" describes you best, write a 1 beside the "I." If you feel the "C" describes you second best, write a 2 beside the "C," and so on.

You will most likely see words in all four descriptions that apply to you, but one or two should resonate more than the others. Again no one tendency is *better* than the other and there is no <u>one</u> category that most teachers *should* be. Some of the most highly successful teachers have high tendencies in "S" or "C" (reserved and calculated), rather than outgoing or talkative. Don't think, "Since I am a teacher, I *should* be a. . ." Be honest about who you really are. When you do, *your stress levels will decrease dramatically*! **(Don't forget to rank as 1, 2, 3, or 4.)**

\_\_\_ **D**=Dominant, Driving, Demanding, Determined, Decisive Doer (Fast-Paced and Task Oriented) Likes to take charge of situations, sometimes it's *"My way or the highway,"* as in *"These are **my** class rules and we aren't voting on them."* Has very few discipline problems in class.

\_\_\_ **I**=Inspirational, Influencing, Interactive, Interested in people (Fast-Paced and People Oriented) Likes to talk and talk and talk. . .Enjoys parties and social events, has a good sense of humor, expresses their ideas, enthusiastic. Usually liked by most students and colleagues.

\_\_\_ **S**=Supportive, Stable, Steady, Submissive, Sometimes Shy (Slow-Paced and People Oriented) Likes to go along with whatever others want, doesn't want to "rock the boat" with new ideas, wants everyone to get along with each other. Very loyal to others and does what is right.

___ **C**=Cautious, Calculating, Concerned, Careful, Competent (Slow-Paced and Task Oriented) Likes to make sure the job is done correctly, may be formal and reserved, double and triple-checks the accuracy of grades or reports turned into the office. Maintains detailed, up-to-date lesson plans.

Do you "see yourself" in the DISC Profile? If you feel two of the categories accurately describe you, then rank them both the same.

As you can see, all temperaments in the DISC assessment have strengths that are important and necessary. Bottom line— you are valuable just as you are. So— Be YOU!

I've found that school faculties have a lot of fun with the DISC Profile. Once everyone understands the main characteristics of each temperament type, they begin to identify their colleagues' tendencies as well as their own.

For example, think of someone on your faculty who comes to school a month before the school year begins to:
- put up all their bulletin boards.
- prepare lesson plans for the entire first semester.
- run copies of all their tests and quizzes for the first grading period.

Maybe this is a *little* exaggeration, but you get the point. These are typical activities accomplished by someone with a high "C" temperament. If you looked up *organized or doing-it-by-the-book* in the dictionary, you would find their picture.

Speaking of fun— yes, learning **should** be enjoyable— let's look at the humorous side of DISC. Learn about yourself and others using DISC, but **have some fun** with it and don't take yourself too seriously. **One of the most effective ways for reducing stress in your life is the ability to laugh at yourself! Go ahead— LAUGH!**

# DISC Humor

## Grocery Shopping and DISC:

**D** - shops impulsively and never makes a list.

**I** - tells you where everything is in the store, whether you ask or not.

**S** - is prepared with a list and goes up and down each aisle making sure everyone she meets is finding what they're looking for.

**C** - walks up and down the aisles with a deliberate strategy, using coupons and a calculator, taking careful notice of those little cards under products that identify the "cost per ounce." C also alerts the cashier if there has been a mistake ringing up the sale.

## Parent-Teacher Conferences and DISC:

**D** - hands the parent the student's final grade and abruptly ends the conference.

**I** - boasts about his/her teacher qualifications, then spends the remainder of the session discussing the student's interaction with others. Hasn't a clue about the student's grades.

**S** - wants to make sure the parents and student "feel okay" about the school, his/her teaching, room temperature. etc.

**C** - provides a printout of every score, worksheet, and paper the student has received the entire school year and a detailed list of each item that was wrong on every quiz and test, and keeps an up-to-date average on every student every day.

We all have at least a "smidgen" of each temperament but we concentrate primarily on one to two. Personally, I have high tendencies as an "I" - I like to talk and talk and talk. . .I also exhibit very low tendencies as an "S" or "C." High "S's" and "C's" say things to me like, "Jerry, you are always on the go, go, go. Your energy is really getting on my nerves. Would you please be quiet, slow down, and for crying out loud stop drinking so much coffee every morning. You *definitely* don't need any caffeine."

*People* with different temperaments than yours can cause you stress! Instead of resenting other temperaments, however, learn to understand how the DISC helps you appreciate their differences. Did you ever think, "I wonder why he/she acts like that? Think about your spouse, children, or friends. In which DISC areas do they exhibit the greatest tendencies? Acknowledging these tendencies can enhance your communication and relationships, and reduce stress at home. With the DISC you can understand how others are motivated to respond, so that you can appreciate and respect his or her differences. The result? You will also experience a more stress-free life at school.

However, our temperaments do not justify inappropriate behavior: "I'm a high D, that's why I can't control my temper," or "I can't help it if I'm unorganized, I'm a high C." The DISC teaches us to identify our limitations as well as our strengths.

## Key Principles of Managing Stress and Teacher Burnout

- Stress is caused by our *perspective* of a situation, not the situation itself.
- We become frustrated and worry about problems because we procrastinate solving them and in our minds make them "bigger than they really are."
- The DISC Profile is used to reduce stress and burnout by showing us that our differences are important and helping us to accept the uniqueness of others.

## Teacher Success Strategies to Strangle Stress and Teacher Burnout

- Take action necessary to solve problems at home. They won't "just go away."
- Be flexible. Go with the flow. Unexpected things *will* happen. Learn to adjust.
- Don't take everything personally, especially the response of others. Everyone is not going to like everything you do or say. It doesn't mean you're a failure. It's just their opinion of you at that moment.
- Use the 5-5-5 guideline for worrying.
- Be prepared. The scout motto relates to *thorough lesson preparation*. Even if you aren't able to accomplish all you wish, the more prepared you are the better you will be able to handle the unexpected. Set daily goals for outside the classroom - a "to-do list"— and *do it!*
- Begin a personal wellness program to improve your physical health. The basics of getting plenty of rest, eating right, and exercising are an important part of reducing stress and becoming the winner you were created to be!
- De-junk your life. Get organized. You can do it. Clean the clutter off your desk, file things that need to be filed, and catch up on grading your papers. **Working *harder* does not reduce stress. Working *smarter* reduces stress.**
- Accept your mistakes when you make them. Not *if you* make them— *when* you make them. Forgive yourself, use it as a learning experience (I have a *lot* of "learning experiences"), and move on to the things that need to be done today!
- Continue your personal plan of improving your self-image and feeding your mind a daily diet of "positive thoughts" by listening to tapes, reading, and surrounding yourself with positive people. . .every day!

- **SMILE!** That's right. You have something to smile about, don't you? Look for something humorous and you'll find it. (Include reading the comics in your daily motivational quiet time). Look for something humorous every day at home and at school and you will find it! Humor and laughter are nature's build-in "stress-busters!"

### Teacher Success Strategy #3
### PLAN OF ACTION

Write (from memory) Teacher Success Strategy #1:

_____

Write (from memory) Teacher Success Strategy #2:

_____

Write (from memory) Teacher Success Strategy #3:

_____

What motivational tape or book will you learn from today?

_____

List two unimportant things you have been worrying about that you will stop worrying about— beginning today.
A. _____      B. _____

Which top two behavior tendencies in the DISC Profile describe you best (D,I,S,C)? _____

Why?_____

What is one specific change you will make to begin living a less stressful life—beginning today? _____

_____

As a result of feeding your mind a daily diet of positive thoughts and accepting yourself as you are (Teacher Success Strategies #1 and #2), you'll also start to experience a less stressful and more productive life (Success Strategy #3)! Don't stop. Practice every day!

> **The road to success is always under construction!**

Please write the following statement: "The first three teacher success strategies are life-changing, and the next three are going to be even better!" _____

_____

_____

By completing and continuing to practice the first three strategies, YOU have reached a major milestone in becoming the highly successful teacher and the winner in life you were meant to be! CONGRATULATIONS!

The first three strategies complete Stage I. Continue practicing them daily as you being Stage II, starting with Teacher Success Strategy #4. So, with your rocket mind now on the launch pad, it's time for lift off!

Are you ready? **Are YOU ready? Ya' gotta mean it when you say it.**

**"YES! I am <u>definitely</u> ready to begin Teacher Success Strategy #4!"**

## Touch Students' Hearts Before
## Teaching Their Minds!

I am a teacher and I find myself asking the same question over and over:

# *Why Do I Do It?*

Most of the time I don't know the answer.

Many times I get tired of waiting for the answer and walk off in frustration. Other times I fall asleep pondering the question. When I am struggling with my checkbook, I ask this question:

### *Why do I do it?*

When I am up at four in the morning so I can finish typing tests and searching for materials (since we don't have books that match our state mandated standardized test, Standards of Learning), I ask myself this question:

### *Why do I do it?*

When I have to stay for meeting after meeting, leaving me no time to fix dinner for my family, I ask myself this question:

### *Why do I do it?*

When the child in the last row throws a pencil at me for the fourth time, I ask myself this question:

### *Why do I do it?*

When I'm at Wal-Mart buying my own children's clothes off the clearance rack so I can afford the needed paper and scissors for school, I ask myself this question:

### *Why do I do it?*

When I spend my evenings taking university classes and my summers at professional-development conferences, I ask myself this question:

*Why do I do it?*

When I have to go to school on Saturdays to do paperwork, I ask myself this question:

*Why do I do it?*

When I hear people blame teachers for the problems in the schools today, I ask myself this question:

*Why do I do it?*

When I hear people say that teachers have it easy because "they have the summer off," I ask myself this question:

*Why do I do it?*

When I'm looking for a second job so that I can afford to go on vacation, I ask myself:

*Why do I do it?*

When I sit waiting after school for a parent who never shows up for the conference, I ask myself this question:

*Why do I do it?*

When I have to go more than six hours without going to the bathroom, let alone eat a lunch without gulping it down, I ask myself this question:

*Why do I do it?*

When I am standing at the copy machine at Kinko's because the school is out of paper, I ask myself this question:

*Why do I do it?*

I ask this question a lot. I often have no answer for it. Recently, one of my children recognized me as her teacher in a very special way and the answer became loud and clear to me.

### *Why do I do it?*

I do it for the children. I do it for those who show appreciation and for those who do not. The same question is always there, and it is a new gift each time it gets answered again.

### *Why do I do it?*

I do it for the children.

by Ann K. Alonso, Teacher

> "One looks back, with gratitude, to those who touched our human feelings. Warmth is the vital element for the growing plant and for the soul of a child."
>
> Carl Jung

# Teacher Success Strategy 4

## TOUCH THEIR HEARTS BEFORE YOU TEACH THEIR MINDS!

*One Friday, in the classroom, things just didn't feel right. We had worked hard on a new concept all week, and I sensed that the students were growing frustrated with themselves— and edgy with one another. I had to stop this crankiness before it got out of hand. So I asked them to list the names of the other students in the room on two sheets of paper, leaving a space between each name. Then I told them to think of the nicest thing they could say about each of their classmates and write it down.*

*It took the remainder of the class period to finish the assignment, but as the students left the room, each one handed me their paper.*

*That Saturday, I wrote down the name of each student on a separate sheet of paper, and I listed what everyone else had said about that individual. On Monday I gave each student his or her list. Some of them ran two pages. Before long, the entire class was smiling.*

*"Really?" I heard whispered. "I never knew that meant anything to anyone!" "I didn't know others like me so much!"*

*No one ever mentioned those papers in class again. I never knew if they discussed them after class or with their parents, but it didn't matter. The exercise had accomplished its purpose. The students were happy with themselves and one another again.*

*That group of students moved on. Several years later, after I had returned from a vacation, my parents met me at the airport. As we were driving home, Mother asked me the usual questions about the trip: how the weather was, my experiences in general. There was a slight lull in the conversation. Mother gave Dad a sideways glance and simply said, "Dad?" My father cleared his throat. "The Eklunds called last night," he began.*

*"Really?" I said. "I haven't heard from them for several years. I wonder how Mark is." Dad responded quietly, "Mark was killed in Vietnam," he said. "The funeral is tomorrow, and his parents would like it if you could attend." To this day I can still point to the exact spot on I-494 where Dad told me about Mark.*

*I had never seen a serviceman in a military coffin before. . .The church was packed with Mark's friends. (His old classmate) Chuck's sister sang "The Battle Hymn of the Republic." Why did it have to rain on the day of the funeral? It was difficult enough at the graveside. The pastor said the usual prayers and the bugler played taps. One by one those who loved Mark took a last walk to the coffin and sprinkled it with holy water.*

*I was the last one to bless the coffin. As I stood there, one of the soldiers who had acted as a pallbearer came up to me. "Were you Mark's math teacher?" he asked. I nodded as I continued to stare at the coffin. "Mark talked about you a lot," he said.*

*After the funeral, most of Mark's former classmates headed to Chuck's farmhouse for lunch. Mark's mother and father were there, obviously waiting for me. "We want to show you something," his father said, taking a wallet out of his pocket. "They found this on Mark when he was killed. We thought you might recognize it."*

*Opening the billfold, he carefully removed two worn pieces of notebook paper that had obviously been taped, folded and refolded many times. I knew without looking that the papers were the ones on which I had listed all the good things each of Mark's classmates had said about him. "Thank you so much for doing that," Mark's mother said. "As you can see, Mark treasured it."*

*Mark's classmates started to gather around us. Chuck smiled rather sheepishly and said, "I still have my list. It's in the top drawer of my desk at home." John's wife said, "John asked me to put his in our wedding album." "I have mine too," Marilyn said. "It's in my diary." Then Vicki, another classmate, reached into her pocketbook, took out her wallet and showed her worn and frazzled list to the group. "I carry this with me at all times," Vicky said without batting an eyelash. "I think we all saved our lists."*

*That's when I finally sat down and cried.*

by Helen P. Mrosla, Teacher

Why do you think adults would save a piece of paper they received in elementary school? Two reasons: 1) People hunger for encouragement and appreciation. 2) A teacher did more than "teach" the content, she touched their hearts. *Highly successful teachers understand that students will work harder for them if they feel appreciated.*

> **Students will forget most of what you teach them, but will remember all of how you made them feel in your class!**

Most of the time we put the cart before the horse. We concentrate on the *teaching* instead of the *touching*. Can you remember a time when your teacher cared more about you as a person than as a student? What a difference encouragement makes!

## Encouraging Words

A group of frogs were traveling through the woods and two of them fell into a deep pit. All the other frogs gathered around the pit. When they saw how deep the pit was, they told the unfortunate frogs they would never get out. The two frogs ignored the comments and tried to jump out of the pit. The other frogs kept telling them to stop, that they were as good as dead.

Finally, one of the frogs took heed to what the other frogs said and simply gave up. He fell down and died. The other frog continued to jump as hard as he could. Once again, the crowd of frogs yelled at him to stop the pain and suffering and just die. But he jumped even harder and finally made it out.

When he got out, the other frogs asked him, "Why did you continue jumping? Didn't you hear us?" The frog explained to them that he was deaf and *thought they were <u>encouraging and cheering</u> him on the entire time!*

The story teaches us two lessons: 1) There is power of life and death in the tongue. An encouraging word to someone who is down can lift them up and help them make it through the day. 2) A destructive word can kill the spirit. Be careful of what you say. Speak life to everyone who crosses your path.

When you make them feel significant, their self-worth and confidence will grow. Special is the teacher who will take the time to encourage another person.

### M.M.F.I. "Make Me Feel Important!"

The Institute of Student Motivation conducted a study that clearly showed the impact of self-confidence on academic achievement is greater than that of IQ!

Building self-esteem is *more* than just making students "feel good." Recent studies by the University of Pennsylvania and the Institute of Student Motivation revealed that self-confidence has a greater impact on academic achievement than IQ. Students with high self-esteem are also more successful in their careers and *get higher paying jobs* than students with low self-esteem.

Many students focus on their limitations rather than their capabilities. Former UCLA basketball coach John Wooden - who won 7 national championships in 10 years - said, *"Don't let what you cannot do interfere with what you can do!"* Encouraging students can prevent them from fearing failure or quitting.

*A dedicated mother wanted to encourage her young son's progress on the piano, so she took him to a concert. After they were seated, the mother spotted a friend in the audience and walked down the aisle to greet her. Seizing the opportunity to explore the wonders of the concert hall, the little boy rose and eventually explored his way through a door marked "NO ADMITTANCE."*

*When the house lights dimmed and the concert was about to begin, the mother returned to her seat and discovered that the child was missing. Suddenly, the curtains parted and spotlights focused on the impressive Steinway on stage. In horror, the mother saw her little boy sitting at the keyboard, innocently picking out "Twinkle Twinkle Little Star."*

*At that moment, the great piano master Paderewski made his entrance, quickly moved to the piano, and whispered in the boy's ear, "Don't quit. Keep playing." Then leaning over, Paderewski reached down with his left hand and began filling in the bass part.*

*Soon his right arm reached around to the other side of the child and added a running obbligato. Together, the old master and the young novice transformed a potentially embarrassing situation into a wonderfully creative experience. The audience was absolutely mesmerized.*

However hopeless we think our students and class situation may be, we must remember that our Creator is whispering deep within our being, "Don't quit. Keep playing. Don't quit. Keep playing."

We also need to encourage our students to remain on their stage and "keep playing."

> **Making students feel significant is a vital part of being a highly successful teacher.**

Students want to please when they're encouraged. Remember: 10% of your students will excel in spite of your encouragement, or lack thereof. They are intrinsically motivated. But the other 90% depend greatly on your ability to nurture and encourage.

A few years ago my sons, Jon and Chris, only pulled for winning sports teams. In the '90's they focused on the highly successful Chicago Bulls. They liked the Bulls because MJ and Company rarely lost. It's only natural for people to associate themselves with winners instead of losers. As teachers, however, you must support the "less successful" as well as the winners.

Your students want to be winners, too, but few have *fans* at home pulling for them. Rarely does Mom stand at the door and greet them saying, "How was your day at school?" When parents finally return for the evening, they're usually so stressed out they often criticize the students and make them feel unimportant. **YOU may be the one person in their life that can give them security and make them feel significant!**

Have you ever taken a class where the teacher really "knew his/her stuff" and it was obvious their intention was to impress everyone with their abundance of knowledge? One of the most important principles of being a highly successful teacher is:

**Students don't care how much you know
until they know how much you care!**

Listening isn't convenient, is it? You probably feel you hardly have time to take care of required responsibilities, much less time to listen to students. Finding time to listen is one of the greatest challenges of highly successful teachers. Most teachers have time to lecture; few make time to listen. Lecture to your students and they'll hear your cause— but listen to them and they'll know you care.

And let's be honest. It's tough to listen to Honor Roll Students, but it's even tougher to find time for non-performers. I've never seen a book on success, morals, or religious guidelines that instructs us to "only treat people with respect, who respect you first."

Teachers who want to make a life-long impact "make" the time: time for the rude as well as the respectful. It's tough but you can do it. Successful teachers do things unsuccessful teachers aren't willing to do. These words say it best:

### The Paradoxical Commandments of Leadership

*People are illogical, unreasonable, and self-centered— love them anyway.*

*If you do well, people will accuse you of selfish, ulterior motives— do well anyway.*

*If you're successful, you'll win false friends and true enemies— succeed anyway.*

*The good you do today will perhaps be forgotten tomorrow— do good anyway.*

*Honesty and frankness make you vulnerable— be honest and frank anyway.*

*The biggest person with the biggest ideas can be shot down by the smallest person with the smallest mind— think big anyway.*

*People favor underdogs but follow only hot dogs— fight for the underdogs anyway.*

*What you spend years building may be destroyed overnight— build anyway.*

*People really need help but may attack you if you help them— help them anyway.*

*Give the world the best you have and you may get kicked in the teeth— give the world the best you have anyway.*

I remember one of my highly esteemed college professors saying to our class during my freshman year in college, "I look forward to learning from you." We couldn't understand what he meant. He was going to learn from *us?* He explained that when we reach a point in life where we as teachers think we know it all and can't learn from our students, it's time to leave the teaching field, go in the locker room, pack our duffel bag, and go home. Always listen for things to learn from your students.

> **"The world talks to the mind. A teacher speaks more intimately; a teacher talks to the heart."**
>
> **Haim Ginott**

The following true story is a powerful example of how adults *can* learn from students—beginning by "touching hearts":

### Sacrifice Play

Chush, a school located in Brooklyn, caters to learning disabled children. Some of these children remain in Chush for their entire school career, while others eventually transfer to conventional schools.

At a fund-raising dinner, the father of a Chush child delivered a speech that would never be forgotten by all who attended. After extolling the school and its dedicated staff, he cried out, "Where is the perfection in my son, Terry?

Everything our Creator does is done with perfection. But my child cannot understand things as other children do. My child cannot remember facts and figures as other children do. Where is our Creator's perfection?"

The audience was shocked by the question, pained by the father's anguish and stilled by the piercing query. "I believe," the father answered, "that when God brings a child like this into the world, the perfection that He seeks is in the way people react to this child— *how they touch his or her heart.*"

He then told the following story about his son Terry:

One afternoon Terry and his father walked past a park where some boys Terry knew were playing baseball. Terry asked, "Do you think they will let me play?" Terry's father knew that his son was not at all athletic and that most boys would not want him on their team.

But Terry's father understood that if his son were chosen it would give him a comfortable sense of belonging and self-worth.

Terry's father approached one of the boys in the field and asked if Terry could play. The boy looked around for guidance from his teammates. Getting none, he took matters into his own hands and said, "We are losing by six runs and the game is in the eighth inning. I guess he can be on our team and we'll try to put him up to bat in the ninth inning."

Terry was told to put on a glove and go out to play short center field. Terry's father was ecstatic as Terry smiled broadly. In the bottom of the eighth inning, Terry's team scored a few runs but was still behind by three. In the bottom of the ninth inning, Terry's team scored again and now with two outs and the bases loaded with the potential winning run on base, Terry was scheduled to be up. Would the team actually let him bat at this juncture and give away their chance to win the game?

Surprisingly, Terry was given the bat. Everyone knew Terry wouldn't get on base. He didn't even know how to hold the bat properly, let alone hit with it. However, as Terry stepped up to the plate, the pitcher moved a few steps to lob the ball in softly so Terry should at least be able to make contact. The first pitch came in and Terry swung clumsily and missed. One of Terry's teammates came up to him and together they held the bat and faced the pitcher, waiting for the next pitch. The pitcher again took a few steps forward to toss the ball softly toward Terry.

As the pitch came in, Terry and his teammate swung the bat and together they hit a slow ground ball to the pitcher. The pitcher picked up the soft grounder and could easily have thrown the ball to the first baseman. Terry would have been out and that would have ended the game. Instead, the pitcher took the ball and threw it on a high arc to right field, far beyond the reach of the first baseman.

Everyone started yelling, "Terry, run to first. Run to first!" Never in his life had Terry "run to first." He scampered down the baseline wide-eyed and startled. By the time he reached first base, the right fielder had the ball. He could have thrown the ball to the second baseman to tag out Terry, who was still running. But the right fielder understood what the pitcher's intentions were, so he threw the ball high and far over the third baseman's head. Everyone yelled, "Run to second. Run to second!"

Terry ran towards second base as the runners ahead of him deliriously circled the bases towards home. As Terry reached second base, the opposing shortstop ran to him, turned him in the direction of third base and shouted, "Run to third." As Terry rounded third, the boys from both teams ran behind him screaming, "Terry, run!"

Terry ran home, stepped on home plate and all 18 boys lifted him on their shoulders. They made him the hero, as if he had just hit a "grand slam" and won the game for his team.

"That day," said the father, with tears now rolling down his face, "those 18 boys reached their level of our Creator's perfection and taught a valuable lesson by 'touching Terry's heart.'"

(Author Unknown)

**Words of encouragement give the power of hope!** When I was a kid, I remember hearing the statement, *"Sticks and stones may break my bones, but words will never hurt me."* Whoever came up with that "brilliant" principle ought to have his head examined! Nothing can be farther from the truth.

A few years ago I spoke at a state conference for 1,400 school administrators. During my talk I said, "As serious as the situation regarding weapons and violence is in our schools today, discouraging words have killed the spirit of more young people than all the guns and knives together."

Afterwards a lady introduced herself, and showed me a picture of her son, in his Junior Varsity football uniform. She expressed her appreciation for my comment about young people and the impact of words.

She continued by telling me how his football coach almost decimated her son's confidence by saying, "You know, you are a fine football player, but you're never going to amount to much on the basketball court." A few words, with a powerful impact.

> **Choose words that help you be a "dream-maker" - not a "dream-breaker!"**

Yes, words are important and what you say will have an impact on students. For fun, let's look at. . .

## 7 Things You Won't Hear Teachers Say

1.  "Our principal is sooooooooo smart. . .no wonder he/she is in administration!"

2.  "I can't believe I actually get paid for doing this!"

3.  "Thank goodness for these evaluations. They really keep me focused!"

4.  "It's Friday? Already? This week has just flown by!"

5.  "All of our in-service training programs are so exciting!"

6.  "We'd be able to better educate our children if they would let us teach through July and only have one week of vacation!"

7.  "My spouse thinks I'm around the house too much and that I'm not spending enough time at school!"

Below are typical comments of what highly successful teachers **are** saying about the importance of touching hearts:

"College didn't prepare me for the student whose mother was murdered by a jealous boyfriend; for the student who witnessed a drive-by shooting; for the student who was removed from his/her home because of an abusive father; or for the student who hasn't eaten since lunch in the school cafeteria the day before. These realities do not exist in the textbooks, yet they are too often the realities that many students bring into my classroom. Students are real people with real problems. *How can you expect them to care about your course content until they know you care about them as a person, with all their hurts in life?*"

## Remember the Children

*Remember the children. . .*
Who sneak Popsicles before supper,
Who erase holes in math notebooks,
Who can never find their shoes,
Who hug us in a hurry and forget their lunch money,
Who spend all their allowance before Tuesday,
Who have temper tantrums in stores and pick at their food,
Who like ghost stories and shove dirty clothes under the bed,
Who never rinse out the tub,
Who squirm in church, and
Who don't like to be hugged or kissed in front of their friends because it's not "cool."

And we remember the children. . .
Who never get dessert,
Who have no safe blanket to drag behind them,
Who can't find any bread to steal,
Who don't have a room to clean up,
Whose pictures aren't on anyone's dresser,

Touch Their Hearts Before
You Teach Their Minds!

Who never went to the circus,
Who live in an X-rated world,
Whose smiles can make us cry,
Whose nightmares come in the daytime,
Who will eat anything,
Who have never been to the dentist,
Who aren't spoiled by anybody,
Who go to bed hungry and cry themselves to sleep,
Who *want* to be carried, and for those who *must* be carried,
Who never give up, and for those who never get a second chance,
And we remember the children. . .
Who will grab the hand of anybody kind enough to offer it!

> **Remember, some of us learn from other people's mistakes and the rest of us have to be the other people.**

Communication is our primary tool to touch students' hearts. But only 7% of our communication is verbal. Our tone of voice and volume, and body posture say more than our words. But what students and others "hear" more than anything is the message we send with our body language.

Can you spare a minute, even though you're running to a faculty meeting, to "hear the heart" of a student whose speech boasts of confidence but whose posture reveals inner struggle? Highly successful teachers connect to their students by listening to them. When a teacher makes this type of effort, in class, you will be amazed how you can transform young people and inspire them to think, feel, and take action— if you will just make the time to *touch their hearts*.

> **"One of the most important things a teacher can do is to send the pupil home in the afternoon liking himself just a little better than when he came in the morning."**
>
> **Ernest Melby**

## STOP, LOOK & LISTEN

Ever hear those familiar words from your mom when you were a kid? Familiar but powerful guidelines that can help us as teachers to connect with our students.

**STOP:** While visiting a school, I saw the following sign on a teacher's desk:

> **"Students aren't an interruption of my work - they are the reason I have my job!"**

Grading papers and completing other paperwork are required tasks. But this statement accurately communicates the necessity of keeping our typical day in perspective. It's easy to gripe about students, but in reality, would you be employed if they weren't enrolled? No matter the tyranny of your "busyness," STOP when a student needs you to listen.

**LOOK:** Sherlock Holmes would often exhort his clients, "You see, but you do not observe." Are you observing the body language and verbal tone of your students? Why not be the teacher that breaks the communication barriers down and gives students a chance to change their lives?

**LISTEN:** The most successful salespeople aren't the "big talkers." Top salespeople listen to their customers' needs. It's the same with highly successful teachers. By the way, you ARE a salesperson— a vital member of the most important sales force in the world.

What does the student really need? Are you asking? Are you listening?

**"Many times, what matters most to a student is how his or her teacher demonstrates caring. Learning happens most effectively when students feel like their teacher has a genuine personal connection with them."**

**from "Personal Connection is Crucial to Learning,"**
**Virginia Journal of Education**
**(March 2001)**

Even when you take the time to STOP, LOOK, and LISTEN, many days you will try— unsuccessfully— to reach those "hard-to-reach" students and will leave school feeling as if you aren't making a difference. On those days (as you know, they seem to come quite often), keep the message of the following story alive in your heart:

*I had a very special teacher in high school many years ago whose husband died unexpectedly of a heart attack.*

*About a week after his death, she shared some of her insight with our class. As the late afternoon sunlight came streaming in through the classroom windows and the class was nearly over, she moved a few things aside on the edge of her desk and sat down there.*

*With a gentle look of reflection on her face, she paused and said, "Before class is over, I would like to share with all of you a thought that is unrelated to class, but which I feel is very important. Each of us is put here on earth to learn, share, love, appreciate and give of ourselves.*

*None of us knows when this fantastic journey experience will end. It can be taken away at any moment. Perhaps this is God's way of telling us that we must make the most out of every single day."*

*Her eyes beginning to water, she went on, "So I would like you all to make me a promise. From now on, on your way to school, or on your way home, find something beautiful to notice. It might be something you see or a scent or something you hear.*

*Please look for these things, and cherish them. For, although it may sound trite to some, these things are the 'stuff' of life. The little things we are put here on earth to enjoy. The things we often take for granted. We must make it important to notice them, for at any time, it can be taken away."*

*The class was completely quiet. We all picked up our books and filed out of the room silently. That afternoon, I noticed more things on my way home from school than I had the whole semester.*

Every once in awhile, I think of that teacher and remember what an impression she made on all of us. As we grow older, it is not the things we did that we often regret, but the things we didn't do.

**I have learned that the teachers who shared themselves made a much greater impact on my life than the teachers who just tried to reach my mind!**

## Teacher Success Strategy #4
## PLAN OF ACTION

From memory, write Teacher Success Strategy #1:

_____

From memory, write Teacher Success Strategy #2:

_____

From memory, write  Teacher Success Strategy #3:

_____

From memory, write Teacher Success Strategy #4:

_____

Write the name, or initials, of one difficult student from each of your classes (or 3 students if you have one class) whose hearts you need to touch.

1. _____
2. _____
3. _____
4. _____
5. _____

List specific steps you'll use to connect with these students.

_____
_____
_____

As suggested in Strategy #1 and #2, what positive tape or book are you using as "input" to build your self-esteem?

_____

Odds are, you've been thinking about those "tough kids" as you read this chapter and wonder what specifically you could do to motivate them, right? I hope so, because that's exactly what *Teacher Success Strategy #5* is all about.

Are you "fired up?" If we expect students to be motivated, it starts with us!

# "Success Notes and Quotes"

# Teacher Success Strategy 5

## MOTIVATE EVERY STUDENT WITH ENTHUSIASM AND HIGH EXPECTATIONS!

I love experiments, don't you? When I took science, experiments were the best part of class. Take a look at this experiment recently conducted concerning teacher expectations and students' learning:

*At Oak Elementary School in San Francisco, a group of teachers were told that they were special teachers who were to be part of a special experiment. The researchers said, "Based on a pretest, we have identified 20 percent of your students who are 'special.' They will be 'spurters' or 'bloomers' and are a designated group of students of whom greater intellectual growth is expected."*

*The names were actually selected at random, but the teachers were led to believe that the status of being "special" children was based on scores on the pretest, the Harvard Test of Inflected Acquisition. "As a special reward for your teaching excellence, we are going to tell you this information, but with two conditions:*

*You must not tell the students that you know that they are special.*

*None of us are going to tell the parents that their children are special.*

*Thus, we expect and know that you will do extremely well with these special students."*

*Eight months later, all the students were tested again, and a comparison was made of the designated special students and the undesignated students, as measured by IQ scores. The results showed a significant gain in intellectual growth for the 20 percent who were designated "special."*

*The administrators brought the teachers in, showed them the growth results of their students, and congratulated them on their spectacular success with their students. The teachers said, "Of course, we had special students to worth with. It was easy, and they learned so fast."*

*The administrators and researcher said, "We'd like to tell you the truth. The so-called 'special' children were picked at random. We made no selections based on IQ or aptitude."*

*"Then it must have been us," said the teachers, "because you said we were special teachers selected to be part of a special experiment." "We need to tell you something else, too," replied the researcher. "All the teachers were involved in this experiment. None of you were designated special over any other teacher."*

*There was only one experimental variable. . .EXPECTATION!*

Source: "The First Days of School,"
Harry K. and Rosemary T. Wong. Rosenthal,
Robert, and Lenore Jacobson. (1968)
"Pygmalion in the Classroom."

> ## Students will perform to the level of expectations of their teacher!

Do you remember Teacher Success Strategy No. 1? (In case you're having "one of those days," let me help: **"Unleash Your Personal Power with a Dynamic Self-Image!"**) One of the most important factors in raising our personal self-esteem is to expect the best of ourselves. This is also a prerequisite to expecting the best in our students.

When students improve their self-esteem, they will begin to have more confidence in themselves and expect more of themselves. But, they need to believe that you're committed to help them rise to a higher level of success.

### If you plan on raising students to the next level, get on higher ground yourself!

Recently, I facilitated a two-day training session for school superintendents. At the beginning of the session I posed this question, "If you could wave a magic wand, what is the first thing you would change about your teachers?" Seventy percent of them stated they had great confidence in their teachers, but wished they had more confidence in themselves and in their students to raise the performance and achievement bar.

Studies show only 10% of students are intrinsically motivated. Most likely you'll spend the bulk of your teaching career with the other 90%. All 100%, however, need understanding and encouragement. Your students are painfully aware of what the world tells them they can't accomplish.

As teachers, we need to focus on what the student *can* accomplish with you this semester or year. Be an encourager and listener and **choose to only expect their best effort— NO EXCEPTIONS!**

Although students may appear to accept or even enjoy classes of teachers with low standards, they actually have more respect for teachers who believe in them enough to demand more, both academically and behaviorally.

In a national survey of 1,300 high school students (Public Agenda, 1997), teens were asked on questionnaires and in focus groups what they think about their teachers and want from them. Their responses are summarized in the following cluster areas:

1. **Desire for Order**: They complained about lax teachers and non-enforced rules. Many feel insulted at the minimal demands placed upon them. They stated unequivocally that, **"they would work harder if more were expected of them."**

2. **Desire for Structure**: They expressed a desire for "closer monitoring and watchfulness from teachers."

Similarly, when 200 middle school students were surveyed about their most memorable work in school, they repeatedly "equated hard work with success, satisfaction, and self-esteem." **They want to be challenged!** (Wasserstein, 1995)

I have observed that nearly all schools "claim" to hold high expectations. However, "saying it and doing it" are two different things. I find that most schools have high expectations of only *a few* of their student segments, and low expectations for most of the other student population.

> **"Learning. . .should be a joy and full of excitement. It is life's greatest adventure: it is an illustrated excursion into the mind of noble and learned men, not a conducted tour through a jail!"**
>
> **Taylor Caldwell**

## Four Comments on Teacher Expectations:

1. "Research clearly establishes that *teacher expectations* do play a significant role in determining how well and how much students learn." (Jerry Bamburg, 1994)

2. "When *teachers believe in students*, students believe in themselves. When those you respect (teachers) think you can— YOU think you can!" (James Raffin, 1993)

3. "The other side of the coin is when students are viewed as lacking in ability or motivation and are *not expected to make significant progress,* they tend to give teachers as little as is expected of them." (Peggy Gonder, 1991)

4. "One characteristic of a highly-effective teacher is they *refuse to alter their attitudes or expectations for their students*— regardless of the students' race or ethnicity, life experiences and interests, gender, and family wealth and stability." (Barbara & Les Omotani, 1996)

> **Expectations, as if by magic, come true!**

## How Teachers Communicate Expectations

*Instructions: Self-assess your own communication practices by placing a check beside habits you've practiced. Please be honest:*

\_\_\_\_\_ 1. Pay less attention to "low expectation" students

\_\_\_\_\_ 2. Seat low-expectation students farther from you

\_\_\_\_\_ 3. Wait less time for low-expectation students to answer questions

\_\_\_\_\_ 4. Criticize low-expectation students *more* frequently for incorrect responses

\_\_\_\_\_ 5. Praise low-expectation students *less* frequently after correct responses

\_\_\_\_\_ 6. Provide low-expectation students with less detailed feedback (written/verbal)

\_\_\_\_\_ 7. Interrupt low-expectation students more frequently

\_\_\_\_\_ 8. Demand less effort from low-expectation students

(Source: Educational Sociology: A Realistic Approach, T. Good and J. Brophy)

In 1997, the New York State Department of Education **put their money where their mouth was** by spending $600,000 for a teacher training program designed to raise teacher expectations of students. The state department believed that changing how teachers view their students— *especially their poor-performing students*— is critical to turning around failing schools. **They believe all students can perform at higher levels if they are taught well by teachers who <u>expect</u> them to succeed.** (1997, The New York Times Company)

**What YOU Can Do. . .**

- Be aware of your body language— smile more, have better eye contact. Also, become more aware of your voice tone - stop. . . moans, groans or "You're never right" verbalizations.
- Rearrange the seating arrangement of your classroom.
- Change seating regularly— at least every grading period.
- Allow more time for poor performing students to answer.
- Give low-expectation students more leadership responsibilities, and coach them through the leadership process.
- Monitor your feelings.
- Recognize **effort** - not just grades.

On the first day of school (or tomorrow, if you are reading this during the school year), tell students <u>what</u> you expect and <u>why</u> you expect their best effort.

**70% of all prisoners were told by a teacher and/or parent that, "One of these days you're going to end up in jail!"**

*Our expectations of students can be life-changing. . .for both the teacher and the student!*

One of my former teachers said to our class on the first day of school, "You've probably heard about me. More students fail my class than pass it and I don't *expect* this group to be any different. I take pride in the fact that I am the toughest teacher in this school. Last semester only two students received an A and one of them possibly should have received a B+. If you pass this class it's because you worked for your grade because I don't <u>give</u> anything."

We agreed with the last statement she made, "She doesn't *give* anything" (including encouragement or help outside the class).

She was telling us **she <u>expected</u> us to fail**! Talk about a serious self-esteem problem— not us— the teacher. Anyone who "fails" students to make her/himself look superior needs to reread Teacher Success Strategy #1, regarding improving their self-esteem. **A highly successful teacher finds joy in helping students experience success— not failure!**

"Okay Jerry," you may say, "I will believe in them and expect their best effort, but tell me how I can motivate those apathetic students who put their heads on their desks and sleep. You know you can't make them learn if they don't want to."

Good point. Earlier we said, *"You can change another person's behavior/performance by helping him/her change the picture of him/herself."* Those apathetic students have a poor picture of themselves and what they can accomplish. Their self-picture may be a result of their parents' lack of attention and negative attitudes. Or it may be a result of past teachers who focused on their negative behavior and held low expectations of their potential.

> **"The most extraordinary thing about a really good teacher is that he or she transcends accepted educational methods."**
>
> **Margaret Meade**

YOU could be the very first teacher to daily demonstrate to those apathetic students that you really do care about them— as people and students! **What an exciting challenge!** The two of you are going to discover their unlimited talents and potential together.

Now that you are working to increase the expectations of ALL your students, it's important to know how to motivate them to accomplish more than they think possible. (They don't *know* what is possible because no one has told them or showed them.)

We know most students begin their formal school experience motivated to learn (sometimes in spite of their parents' attitude). Students have a natural desire to learn and most of them have high expectations for success.

Preschoolers are propelled by curiosity to explore new things and learn. Even when they fail the first few attempts at something, they will keep trying.

Why does this passion for learning decrease to the point of "hating school?" Why do over 25% of all students in the United States quit school before graduating? **They don't believe people care whether they are successful or not.** Show them you DO care about them and expect their best effort every day!

If you have any doubt about this, I suggest you ask a kindergarten teacher in your school or school division if you could drop by sometime to be a "fly on the wall" and observe the anticipation of learning in the eyes and actions of their students. When their teacher asks a question, almost all of the children's hands immediately go up accompanied by exclamations of, "I know, I know" or "Pick me, pick me."

For most learners, motivation and optimism diminish with repeated failure. After a few years, teachers begin to encounter unmotivated students. Once students begin to believe they cannot be successful, teachers begin to hear comments such as, "I don't want to do this," "I don't care," or "I hate school." When you hear students make statements such as these, **don't believe them**. It's easier for them to say they don't care and hate school. If they don't do well, they can save face with their peers because they "didn't try anyway." But if they try and then fail, they lose status and "respect" from their classmates.

Sadly, many teachers accept this "no-care attitude" and lower their expectations of students. **Make a commitment to focus on apathetic students and bring them up to their level of potential instead**

**of them bringing you down to their level of expectations of themselves!**

Can you reach all of them? Probably not. But what about all those you can reach and with whom you *can* make a difference? Your awareness of students' attitudes and beliefs about learning potential can help reduce student apathy.

Some of the biggest factors that influence a student's motivation include:

- home environment (parents' attitudes).
- their peer's beliefs about the importance of education.
- the school setting, classroom environment (Teacher Success Strategy #6— next chapter— will give you tons of great tips for improving this).
- the teacher— YOU!

The apathetic student, as well as the hyperactive student, can be motivated to learn through both intrinsic and extrinsic motivation.

Effective extrinsic motivation to encourage learning often results in the start of intrinsic motivation for a student. In other words, daily encourage your students and they will eventually identify that they can "do it on their own."

**Learn to approach your students differently based on their personality type. Use the information you learned with the DISC assessment in Teacher Strategy #3.** This does NOT mean you must spend extra time with each student. You don't *have* any extra time. It *does* mean that your students are motivated differently based on the characteristics of their temperaments.

Using DISC allows the teacher to recognize predictable patterns of behavior, work together in harmony to create a "win-win" situation for you to motivate your students.

**A Typical Classroom Scenario:**

(Source: Positive Personality Profiles, Robert A. Rohm, 1993)

The teacher stands up, ready to begin his lesson. Because he is unaware of the different behavior tendencies of his students (DISC), he is already at a disadvantage in trying to motivate them.

He asks, "Who discovered America?" Ricky— a high "D"— bursts out, "Columbus!" The teacher frowns and says, "Ricky, you didn't even raise your hand." Ricky replies, "You asked a question so I though you wanted an answer."

Again the teacher asks, "All right, who discovered America?" Yvonne— a high "I"— shoots her hand up and down, waving her arm side to side, and replies, "Could you give me a hint?" The teacher thinks to himself, "How could this student raise her hand and not know the answer?" (What the teacher, who is unfamiliar with the motivation techniques of DISC doesn't realize is, what Yvonne really heard the teacher say was, *"Would someone like to talk?"*). The teacher strolls over to Jamie's desk. She has to call on Jamie— the high "S"— because Jamie never raises his hand. When she asks Jamie, he replies, "Well, in reading over this material and doing my homework last night, it seems— I may be wrong and I don't want to offend anyone, and if anyone wants to disagree with me that's okay, or if someone wants to take my turn I'll let them because I have probably already taken too long— but I think. . .was it Columbus?" The teacher thinks, "Why is this student so shy and intimidated?"

Then the teacher quizzes Susan— the high "C"— and Susan responds, "Who discovered America. . .I'm not sure I understand the question. Do you want me to say Columbus? Before Columbus came, the Indians were here, and before the Indians, the Vikings. So, I'm not sure I understand the question." The teacher is thinking, "Why doesn't someone just answer my simple question?"

**The truth is, all the students <u>are</u> answering the question— but in their own way.**

## How You Can Motivate Students Using "DISC":

### D – "Determined" Student:

direct/straightforward
high self-confidence
competitive
can be domineering
strong desire to reach their goals
likes to lead

*How to Motivate High "D's"*: Let them know it's okay to verbalize their feelings in a polite manner— according to your classroom management guidelines. Let them know it's okay when they don't reach their goals the first time they try.

### I— "Interactive" Student:

talks and talks and talks. . .
outgoing
good sense of humor and personality
wants to be liked and noticed
energetic
creative
may be disorganized

*How to Motivate High "I's"*: Put instructions in writing— even something simple. Allow them to have fun once in a while. They are fast-paced and easily bored. Listen to them.

## S –"Steady/Softhearted" Student:

reserved

loyal

may be shy

wants things to stay the same; doesn't like changes in standard policies such as classroom rules, procedures, or grading

likes to be part of "the group"

*How to Motivate High "S's":* If changes are necessary, explain why. More than any other type of student, you will need to "seek out" these individuals and help them become a part of the class without embarrassing them.

## C— "Conscientious" Student

consistent

likes to be correct and accurate

will complete assignments exactly as the teacher requests

probably have projects completed before they are due

can be a perfectionist; sets high standards for themselves— sometimes too high; doesn't handle criticism very well

*How to Motivate High "C's":* Allow them to ask questions— they will certainly have them— without making them feel stupid or laughed at. Allow them adequate time to respond to your questions. Show respect for their high quality of work by writing a personal note on their paper. "Captain Conscientious" takes even more price in doing it "right" than "Sergeant Soft-heart." If you need help with "numbers," this is your person.

The DISC assessment works both at home and in the classroom. The purpose is not to categorize students in "slots," but recognize that students— like teachers— are different. They recognize, therefore require, different approaches to motivation.

Apply the analytical and motivational tools of the DISC with the exciting tips below. Focus on the strategies you CAN apply in your classroom— don't worry about the ones you can't use. If you want to see different results— *motivated students*— you must try different approaches.

## Mammoth Methods of Motivation!

1. BE ENTHUSIASTIC. . .BE ENTHUSAISTIC. . .BE ENTHUSIASTIC! Just in case you missed number one and aren't sure what the most effective way of motivating students is— **BE ENTHUSIASTIC!** If YOU aren't excited about your class, can you really expect your students to be motivated? As the old saying goes, "You cannot impart what you do not possess." Believe that they can be motivated. It takes time and lots of effort, but YOU can do it. **Visualize those unmotivated, apathetic students as being excited about learning. Don't give up on them!! You may be the very first teacher who shows you care.**

2. BE PREPARED! The Scout's Motto is applicable in motivating students to learn. Enter your classroom with a firm understanding of what you want and what you expect.

3. BE AVAILABLE - Meet one-on-one with students— *especially* those who are apathetic, cause discipline problems, and/or refuse to complete assignments. (In other words, talk to the students you don't *want* to talk to!)

4. BE SPECIFIC - Tell students exactly what they need to do to succeed in your class. Assure them they can do well and you will be there to help them every day.

5. Keep your expectations high but not unrealistic. When students know that no matter how hard they work they won't

meet your expectations, it has a reverse affect - they will be even less motivated than ever!

6. Gradually increase the difficulty of the class requirements. This allows students to experience success early.

7. Be creative. Remember— it's fun to experiment.

8. Give them feedback as soon as possible. Nothing demotivates a student faster than to work on a project or study for a test and then the teacher takes several days to grade and return it.

9. **Recognize effort— not just grades!** Write positive comments on assignments.

10. Find out your students' personal interests. **Suggestion**: give each student an index card for personal information. Ask them to include details like: the name of their favorite dessert, name of their favorite music group, favorite sports team, the food they dislike the most, what they would do first if they won a million dollars, happiest day of their life, and what are their activities in and out of school. (It really surprises teachers to find out sometimes the "quietist kid in class" is president of their 4-H Club or church youth group). When you ask the class questions, make sure you include your own answers. My favorite answer for the topic "food I dislike the most" is "brown, mushy bananas that stick on your knife when you try to slice them— yeech!" This exercise helps them see you as a real person. This is a great way to let students know you care about them. Wrap a rubber band around the cards and refer to their card before meeting with them individually or in preparation for a parent-teacher conference. Don't bring the card to the meeting, read it prior to your conference. (Parents don't know about your "secret

file" and will be impressed that you know their child on a personal basis).

11. Give them some type of out-of-class assignment on a regular basis. Some classes and grades require more home assignments than others, but every class in every school should require students to be accountable. Also, look for special current events programs on television that relate to your class content. As much as we complain about television, if we look for useful information, we can find it. Relating your class to the "real world" motivates students. They are able to see "why" they are learning.

12. Write the year of graduation on the board or somewhere in your classroom so students will see it. Example: Graduation Date Celebration— June 2011. If you are a secondary teacher with students of different grade levels, write all graduation dates. For example: Senior Graduation Date Celebration— June 2004, Junior Graduation Date Celebration— June 2005, etc. Seeing their date of graduation every day is an effective motivating technique. I periodically ask the class to say it out loud, as a group, to further plant this goal in their minds.

---

**If you don't know where you're going, you'll probably end up somewhere else!**

---

**Instructions:** Reread each motivational method listed above and *highlight 3 techniques* you will put into action— immediately! Use the specific tools given in Teacher Success Strategy #1— *"Unleash Your Personal Power with a Dynamic Self-Image!"*— and the tips from Teacher Success Strategy #2— *"Change Your Thinking and You Can Change Your Life!"*— to help you build your own confidence and enthusiasm. Whatever you do— Be Enthusiastic! Write the 3 motivational methods you highlighted and will use below:

1._____
2._____
3._____

Motivating students will require a consistent plan and a caring attitude. The results can be "life-changing". . .both for your students and YOU!

Arrive at class prepared each day, expecting every student's best effort and I promise you will begin to see dramatic changes in your students and yourself. It won't happen overnight, or even in one grading period, but make a decision and a commitment not to give up on anyone and it will happen— sooner than you think!

## Key Principles of Motivating Every Student with Enthusiasm and High Expectations!

- Expect and accept only the best effort of ALL students!
- Be enthusiastic and prepared. . .every day!
- Apply the motivational principles of DISC!
- Never, never, never, never. . .give up on any student!

## Teacher Success Strategy #5
## PLAN OF ACTION

Write, from memory, Teacher Success Strategy #1:

_____

Write, from memory, Teacher Success Strategy #2:

_____

Write, from memory, Teacher Success Strategy #3:

_____

Write, from memory, Teacher Success Strategy #4:

_____

Write, from memory, Teacher Success Strategy #5:

_____

Write the names, or initials, of 3 students you will individually begin to mentor as part of implementing your Motivational Plan of Action. . . .NOW!

1._____2._____   3._____

What tape or book are you using for your own personal inspiration?

_____

**Only one more strategy before you begin your 10-Day Personal Plan of Action! We're almost there. Our last strategy,** *"Create a Classroom of Excellence and Excitement!,"* **is the most dynamic be-**

cause you're going to combine Teacher Success Strategies #1 through #5 to get students excited about learning and life!

I just want to know. . . ARE YOU READY?

# I <u>Know</u> You Are!

# Let's Go!

# "Success Quotes & Notes"

# Teacher Success Strategy

## CREATE A DYNAMIC CLASSROOM OF EXCELLENCE AND EXCITEMENT!

As a first year teacher, I heard the veteran teachers refer to a nightmare they all experienced called "being observed." I suffered no surprise attacks throughout the Fall, and just as I convinced myself I'd slide safety through Christmas break, Mr. Evaluator Administrator entered my world.

He strode to an empty desk in the back of the room, already scribbling on his "Jerry's infractions" yellow pad. I didn't think it was a good sign he started writing before he even sat down!

Teachers described Mr. Evaluator Administrator (MAE for purposes of discussion) as the "Candid Camera Man," because "sometime, somewhere, when you least expect it" he would throw your classroom door open as if to say, "Smile, today is YOUR day to be evaluated! You DO have your lesson plans prepared for the next 17 years, don't you?"

Grasp the full picture of this situation. First, MAE joined me in a class designated as *General Business*. To this day, I firmly believe the Guidance Department reviewed the entire school enrollment and said, "Let's see, she missed 74 days of school last year and probably won't graduate; put her in General Business." You get the picture. I taught four classes of students who were not exactly motivated to become great pillars of the community.

The day Mr. Evaluator Administrator blessed us with his presence, I was doing what any dedicated teacher would be doing— TEACHING! No last day parties during instructional time for me. (Luckily, I had had my Christmas parties three days earlier.)

It didn't take Sherlock Holmes to determine why he was scribbling notes faster than a scribe with the hives. **I was standing on top of my desk, wearing a complete Santa Claus suit - including beard, hat and boots!!** So there I was, a first year teacher, my first observation and evaluation, and I'm standing in front of my class dressed up like Santa Claus. When MAE strode through the door, let's just say my first reaction wasn't "HO HO HO." With no trap door to drop through, I had no choice but to continue teaching as if this were a "normal" situation.

Except for a student yelling, "Mr. King, you're not going to give us homework today just to impress that old man in the back row, are you?", the class went about as well as could be expected.

As I was taking off my beard and Santa hat, he approached me and said, "Could you come by my office for a few minutes after school today to discuss your evaluation?" I wanted to reply, "Actually, Mr. Little Larry Legal Pad, I have already made plans to be home by 4:00 so I can watch a rerun of the *Andy Griffith Show.*"

Instead of telling me how crazy I was for practicing such unorthodox teaching antics (and that I needed to clean out my desk and turn in my room key), he told me I did something that day that many teachers have never done: *I brought my unique personality inside the classroom and used it to reach a very hard-to-reach group of students. He told me to continue to "be myself" and use creative teaching strategies **to create a classroom of excellence and excitement.***

His encouragement to step outside my comfort zone and use a variety of "terrific teaching tools and techniques" was exactly what I needed to hear.

This chapter includes practical and effective tips from highly effective teachers that can help you **Create A Classroom of Excellence and Excitement**. As I have emphasized throughout this book, don't just read it— "do" it. Use your highlighter and/or ink pen as you read and mark the techniques you feel fit your style and personality. Don't be afraid to step out of your comfort zone and try things you haven't tried before.

**Remember: If you are not satisfied with your current results— low-performing, apathetic, or discipline-challenging students— you MUST change what you are doing!!** *"If you keep doing what you've been doing, you're gonna keep getting what you've got!"* What are the most effective teaching methods?

### Teaching Methods and Average Retention Rate
- Lecture - 5%
- Reading - 10%
- Audiovisuals - 20%
- Demonstrate - 30%
- Discussion Groups - 50%
- Practice by doing - 75%
- Students involved in teaching others - 80%

List the least effective method of teaching:

_____

(If you wrote "Lecture" you are correct).

Please list what method you think is most widely used by teachers: _____

(If you wrote "Lecture" again, you are "two for two.")

## Students forget 90% of what they hear during a lecture within 10 hours!

If teachers were truly interested in improving learning and test scores, why would they use the method that is **least effective** for learning? There are many reasons, but one of the leading factors is we "tend to teach the way we have been taught." If you and I were taught by teachers who relied on the lecture method, it's only natural we would follow in their footsteps. Just because *they* used the lecture method, however, doesn't mean it's effective.

Highly successful teachers are willing to try things outside their comfort zones, using a variety of teaching techniques to help students learn as quickly as possible and improve their long-term retention rate. Why is it important to use a variety of teaching techniques?

---

**The average attention span of a high school student is only 12-14 minutes!**

---

As one teacher told me, **"Teachers *covering* it and students *containing* it may be two completely different things."**
- *Master the Principles of Effective Classroom Management*
- *Apply the Principles of Accelerated Learning*

### Principles of Effective Classroom Management:

How much time during a typical day do you spend disciplining students who disrupt your teaching? How about the time you spend doing non-teaching chores such as calling roll and returning papers?

*Research says teachers spend an average of one-third of their time in class with such activities.* Think about how much more teaching and learning could take place by simply managing our class time more effectively.

I highly recommend a book written by Harry K. and Rosemary T. Wong, *"The First Days of School."* It contains this useful information plus many additional suggestions on becoming a highly successful teacher.

## "The #1 factor governing student learning is classroom management!"

(Wong, Dec. 1993, "What Helps Students Learn." Ed. Leadership, pp 74-79)

If you sincerely want to have a *classroom of excellence and excitement*, practice classroom management procedures— beginning the first day of school. You need to practice and rehearse the procedures you want your students to follow— some of them over and over until they get it right. You should rehearse your desired classroom procedures— beginning the first day of school— BEFORE discipline problems occur.

**First Day of School:**

1.   Prepare a seating chart before students arrive. Assign seats to students using an overhead projector or a master seating chart. Each class diagram will take you about 5 minutes to prepare but will save you hours in correcting possible discipline situations. If you don't use charts or overheads, be creative and come up with your own way of doing it! Older students don't like being told where to sit, but using a seating chart will help you learn students' names, check attendance without "calling roll" and separate possible discipline problems. Unless you have an unusual situation, **don't allow stu-**

**students to "sit where they want to."** Also, change their seating arrangement periodically.

2.   Greet students as they arrive and have a short assignment on the board so they immediately begin working. It may be something as simple as filling out a form. I write three things in a special place on the board— every day: 1. A Positive Power Thought for the Day, 2. A trivial question that relates to the subject content, 3. A short class assignment.

3.   When introducing rules: give them a written copy, have the rules and consequences posted in the room, and ask students to repeat them out loud. Repetition enhances memory. Try not to have more than 3-5 *classroom* rules. These rules are in addition to school or school district rules and include areas such as respect for other students, etc.

4.   **Important!** *Procedures and routines must be rehearsed.* Explain exactly how you want certain things done. Be very specific. For example, many teachers allow their students to turn in their test as they finish. Every time a student gets out of his/her seat to walk to the desk, he/she disrupts and distracts other students who are trying to finish their tests. As more students finish, the noise level tends to increase. I found when I enforced the rule of "absolutely no talking" until I take up all tests after everyone is finished or you will receive a zero and allowed them to work on something else when they finished, everyone stayed quiet until the last person finished.

*Possible Additional Procedures and Routines:*
- Taking roll
- Absences and tardies
- Asking questions/need help
- Being excused from the classroom

- Fire drills
- Taking tests
- Beginning of class
- Watching an audio-visual
- Getting into small groups

Explaining and rehearsing will save you a lot of time and headaches. After classroom management, the second important prerequisite to having a classroom of excellence and excitement is to apply the basic principles of Accelerated Learning.

There are many knowledgeable authors in this area, but I highly recommend a book written by Dave Meier, *"The Accelerated Learning Handbook."*

> **"Teachers, students, parents, and communities should stick together. Remember: the banana gets skinned only when it gets away from the bunch."**

## Principles of Accelerated Learning:

Accelerated Learning has one aim: **To get results**! When you apply these principles, your students will learn faster, remember it longer and enjoy learning more. There is a place for enjoyment and a place for seriousness. Teachers and students need both. Suggestion: Highlight the basic principles of areas in which you need to improve.

### Accelerated Learning Basics

- Approach every teaching strategy with an open mind.
- Stop using the "Pour and Snore" technique. This style is characterized by an "I tell, you listen" teaching format. Students learn better in a relaxed and stimulating environment.

- Learning is not a spectator sport. Students don't need to watch the teacher perform. Students learn better when they are actively involved in the learning process.
- All good learning includes collaboration.
- Students learn best when there are a variety of learning options.
- Students learn best when they see *how* the information is used and possibly affects them (Contextual Learning).
- Students learn best when learning involves both mind and the body— that means they need to **MOVE!**

Don't just sit there. . .DO SOMETHING!

Remember that a student has a 12-14 minute attention span. Learning is hampered when we separate the body and the mind. The mind falls asleep when there is no chance for some kind of physical involvement. *Moving allows blood to flow to the brain and helps us learn faster!* A 15-20 second stand-and-stretch break can accomplish wonders. It helps students refocus on what we want them to learn.

**Here are 4 essential phases of a class session. Perform all 4 successfully, and you've got a formula for success.**

1. *Preparation*— arouse students' interest and give them positive feelings about what you are going to teach.

2. *Presentation*—make the learning material interesting; use a *variety* of teaching strategies (as opposed to mostly "lecture").

3. *Practice*— help students incorporate their new knowledge via hands on, problem solving, teams, etc.

4. *Performance*— help students apply and extend their knowledge by reaching past the classroom experience.

Highly effective teachers understand and use the **"SAVI"** principle of Accelerated Learning as often as possible:

**S** = Somatic - Learn by moving and doing
**A** = Auditory - Learn by talking and hearing
**V** = Visual - Learn by observing and with mental pictures
**I** = Intellectual - Learn by problem solving

---

**Break Out of Your Comfort Zone with
Accelerated Learning!**

---

So, what's the difference between a highly effective teacher, one who uses the result-proven teaching strategies of Accelerated Learning, and a teacher who just "covers the material?"

| _Traditional Learning_ | _Accelerated Learning_ |
|---|---|
| Rigid | Flexible |
| Controlling | Nurturing |
| Mental (cognitive) | Mental/Physical/Emotional |
| Time-Based | Results-Based |
| Serious/Somber | Joyful |

Did you read that last one? The difference between being serious and somber and being joyful! Jerry, you mean it's okay to "enjoy" teaching and learning?

**The days of "Don't Smile Until Christmas" for teachers
went out with the horse and buggy!**

"School is _not_ a place for enjoyment and fun," a staff development speaker shared with our teachers. This statement was made at the beginning of an all-day, six-hour training session where he told 43 funny one-liners, jokes, or funny stories! If humor wasn't important in teaching and learning, why did he use it all day to keep our attention? Apparently, it's a great technique for teaching teachers but not for teaching students.

Think about the last speaker or minister you heard. What was their "main point?" If you're like most people, we've forgotten it by the time we return home— many times before we leave the parking lot! Odds are, if we remember anything about what someone says, we remember the humor. Should all teaching and classes be loaded with humor? Of course not. But teachers who don't include an interesting story or humor to help students retain knowledge are leaving out a very effective way of improving long-term retention and test scores.

Creativity, joy, and humor help teachers connect with students. I'm not referring to telling jokes or being a "funny person." I'm suggesting that you create an atmosphere where students don't feel threatened or embarrassed if they make a mistake or say something wrong. Humor can go a long way to help you create such an environment.

One of the most requested in-service programs I provide is *"Learning 'n Laughing."* In this session I offer principles concerning humor and teaching, including:

**Using joy, creativity, and humor in the classroom is NOT:**
- Telling jokes
- Losing control of classroom discipline
- Teaching less subject matter
- Adding preparation time to lesson plans

**Benefits of using joy, humor, and creativity:**
- Builds rapport between students and the teacher
- Maintains a high attention level
- Increases long-term retention
- Promotes divergent thinking

- Enhances self-esteem
- Creates a positive learning environment

The following suggested list is a result of personal interviews with highly successful educators who share their dynamic classroom teaching strategies. Look for and highlight the strategies you can and *will* use. Step out of your comfort zone and— DO IT! Using these tools and techniques will enable you to *Create a Classroom of Excellence and Excitement!*

## Creative Classroom Strategies from Highly Successful Teachers

### (Most are National Board Certified)

With a little imagination and a few changes, you can use these ideas at every level of teaching.

"Use a karaoke machine (or CD/tape player) and play oldies. Use a camera. If you have access to a digital camera, children can have their own disks. I use a digital camera to illustrate action. After the pictures have been taken, the students print them and write about the pictures. Photos can be incorporated into holiday cards for parents, also. Hold class meetings and let students air their frustrations and learn to solve problems. Allowing them to have a part in classroom rules and activities teaches them about the democratic process and gives them ownership into their classroom as a community. Music sets a positive tone in class (when appropriate) and also between classes, as students are leaving and/or arriving. Students are motivated to work for teachers who care enough to display pictures of their students in the classroom."

**Judy Berry**

"It's important for a teacher to like his/her students and the subject matter being taught. Students experience a personal reaction to real life when we do projects involving the economy. One of the classroom projects we do is use cardboard to construct buildings and build a town (businesses, public buildings, etc.). Before the students' very eyes, they see that when factories lay people off, businesses possibly close and homes are foreclosed. But, in the upswing economy there is hope for more demand for new houses and businesses. (Think of the practical writing, reading and speaking experiences you could create from this or another 'building' project in your classroom. Build a theater, build a math or science model, etc.)"

**Bill Holloway**

"Don't be afraid to try simple ideas and hands-on activities with high school students. When I'm having a frustrating day with a student, I try to remember something about that student I appreciate or like. This helps me keep my perspective."

**Susanne Dana**

"I dress as a favorite character— it forces research and investigation. We have Internet Scavenger Hunts. They take some time to plan but are terrific for lower-level learners. The possibilities are endless."

**Nancy Muncie**

"I make an effort to keep kids out of a *cognition coma*. It all started when I was a student teacher. We were studying ancient Egypt and I decided to mummify a chicken. We used a clear jar so the kids could watch the change. In the meantime, we had an archeological dig in the woods outside the school. The students found "ancient" Egyptian relics - bones and other things I had planted under leaves and sticks. Two months later the chicken was mummified and the kids were still talking about Egypt. Today I use a technique I call *'contagious cognition.'* We don't 'study' anything in my class. Instead, the kids get to 'be' people, such as judges, lawyers, and even teachers. 'Being' civics beats 'studying' it. I thank parents and tell them I couldn't do what I do without the help of their child. *Teaching is a team effort. I'm the coach."*

**John Gleason**

"The most important thing a teacher can do is be a facilitator to the students. The student should not perceive the teacher as 'know all, holder of knowledge.' Foster a climate of 'community' in the classroom that works to support one another's learning. This community can only be built and supported by mutual trust and respect."

**Donna Keck**

"I often put lists or sequences to music. For example, to learn how light passes through different parts of the eye, we acted out each motion and as a class chanted: 'Cornea-Pupil-Iris-Lens-Retina-Optic Nerve,' etc. We use tunes everyone is familiar with. Eighty-six students took the test on the eye and 83 did it correctly without a hitch! (I'm pretty sure the other 3 were absent the day we acted it out). The best part is hearing all of the humming during the test! I love it! Students love music. If you are not musically inclined, odds are most of your students will amaze you with their ability of putting information they need to memorize to either nursery rhyme songs or 'appropriate' rap, rock or country tunes."

**Michael Lester**

"Students test which dishwashing detergent blows the biggest bubbles. Test by dipping a straw in the solution and blowing a bubble on a wet surface. Results can be written and/or graphed. Have students observe something and keep a diary about how things change - for example, Moon Diaries. As a writing process use: **P.O.W.E.R.** (Plan, Organize, Write, Evaluate, Revise). Also, we play a learning game called SURVIVAL, using life cards (fire, disease, animals, etc.)."

**Tammy Bowers**

"A good sense of humor and lots of laughter makes for a warm, inviting classroom environment. Teacher expectations for behavior and academic success must be clearly understood. Interactive units are always a hit. I use every opportunity possible to give the students situations to experience real life. Assign groups to work together as much as possible to mixing abilities and personalities. Assign each person a job (note taker, leader, artist, monitor, etc.). No matter what the subject, effective teaching involves consistency, organization, creativity, a sense of humor and above all, fairness and mutual respect."

**Mary Blake**

**My personal summary of the exciting teaching strategies above is:**

**S** top
**T** eaching
**R** eruns
**A** nd
**T** hrust
**E** nthusiastic/Educational
**G** enius
**I** nto
**E** very
**S** ubject

**"And in closing. . ."**

I'm not using this familiar phrase as a "false alarm." We are nearing the end of this part of our success journey together.

Because you made a commitment to read and "do" the strategies in this book, you are already experiencing positive changes in your life. You possess all the necessary character traits needed to become a highly successful person and teacher.

I would like to share a story I heard a few years ago because it had a life-changing impact on my success journey. It is a true story, titled *"Acres of Diamonds."*

A farmer in Africa heard about other farmers getting rich by finding diamonds in rivers and became so excited he sold his farm to go look for these *Acres of Diamonds*. He spent the next thirty years traveling, looking unsuccessfully for the diamonds. He eventually became so discouraged he threw himself in a river and drowned.

Meanwhile, back at the ranch, or in this case the farm, the man who bought his farm was crossing a stream and saw a large, sparkling stone in the water. He picked it up, admired it, and put it on his fireplace mantle where it served as a great conversation piece for visitors in his home. Several weeks later, a visitor asked him if he knew what he had found. The farmer told him he thought it was a piece of crystal because even though the other stones weren't as large as this one, his riverbed was full of such stones.

The farm the farmer had sold to this man turned out to be the most productive diamond mine on the African continent!

**Important lessons teachers can learn:**

- To be a winner in life and in the classroom, we must *expect* to win and *prepare* to win. The farmer didn't take the time or energy to learn what a diamond even looked like.
- We should first look at what we already have, before looking in other places or at other people.

- Each of us is standing— right now— in our own *Acres of Diamonds*. Some of your greatest "riches" in life are sitting in desks every day in your classroom, waiting for you to guide and lead them to success. All we need to do is explore these riches and seek to develop these "rough diamonds," instead of looking elsewhere.
- Your mind is one of your greatest resources. In order to experience a richer, more meaningful life, **you must be willing to change.** To be a "diamond miner" you have to break away from the crowd. To become a highly successful teacher, you cannot be satisfied with being "average."
- Opportunities for success are all around you. Look at your world - your family and students - with new eyes!

**You are living and working in *Acres of Diamonds!*** Understand you have everything you need within yourself to become the highly successful teacher and person you were created to be. Begin today! Put your plan of action in gear to reach your dreams! And whatever you do:

Don't ever. . .ever. . .ever. . .ever. . .ever. . .quit!

**YOU CAN DO IT!**

## "I Am A Teacher"

I am a teacher!

I was born the first moment that a question leaped from the mouth of a child.

The names of those who have practiced my profession ring like a hall of fame for humanity. . .Booker T. Washington, Buddha, Confucius, Ralph Waldo Emerson, Moses and Jesus.

I have wept for joy at the weddings of former students, laughed with glee at the birth of their children, and stood with head bowed in grief and confusion by graves dug too soon for bodies far too young.

Throughout the course of a day I have been called upon to be an actor, friend, nurse and doctor, coach, finder of lost articles, money lender, taxi driver, psychologist, substitute parent, salesman, politician, and keeper of the faith.

Despite the maps, charts, formulas, verbs, stories, and books, I have really had nothing to teach, for my students really have only themselves to learn, and I know it takes the whole world to tell who you are.

I am a paradox. I speak loudest when I listen the most. My greatest gifts are in what I am willing to appreciatively receive from my students.

Material wealth is not one of my goals, but I am a full-time treasure seeker in my quest for new opportunities for my students to use their talents and in my constant search for those talents that sometimes lie buried in self-defeat.

I am the most fortunate of all who labor.

A doctor is allowed to usher life into the world in one magic moment. I am allowed to see that life is reborn each day with new questions, ideas and friendships.

An architect knows that if he builds with care, his structure may stand for centuries.

A teacher knows that if he builds with love and truth, what he builds will last forever.

I am a warrior, daily doing battle against peer pressure, negativity, fear, conformity, prejudice, ignorance, and apathy. But I have great allies: Intelligence, Curiosity, Parental Support, Individuality, Creativity, Faith, Love, and Laughter all rush to my banner with indomitable support.

And whom do I have to thank for this wonderful life I am so fortunate to experience, but you the public, the parents. For you have done me the great honor to entrust to me your greatest contribution to eternity— your children.

And so I have a past that is rich in memories. I have a present that is challenging, adventurous, and fun because I am allowed to spend my days with the future.

I am a teacher. . .and I thank God for it every day!

**John W. Schlatter**

# "I touch the future. I teach."

Christa McAuliffe, American Teacher

**"Success Notes & Quotes"**

# 10-Day Personal Power Plan of Action for Highly Successful Teachers!

(To be completed only after learning
Teacher Success Strategies #1 - #6)

This is <u>your</u> personal plan for applying "The 6 Dynamic Strategies of Highly Successful Teachers" in <u>your</u> life! Make a commitment to complete your *10-Day Personal Power Plan of Action* EVERY DAY before you begin your teaching responsibilities. Don't *have* the time? I encourage you to *make* the time! This is the most important 5 minutes of your day. Highly successful teachers know they must be positively mentally prepared for the challenges of their teaching day. Don't let anything take priority over completing this action plan each day.

## "Home Play"
(You already have too much homework)

In addition to completing your *"10-Day Personal Power Plan of Action"* each morning, I highly recommend you read or listen to one of the books/books-on-tape listed below. Use "Automobile University" to stay motivated. Turn your radio off and play an inspirational tape while traveling to and from school each day. It WILL make a positive difference in your life!

### Video/Audio/Book Resources
- Awaken the Giant Within - Anthony Robbins
- Don't Sweat the Small Stuff - Richard Carlson
- Live Your Dreams - Les Brown
- Success Through A Positive Mental Attitude - Napoleon Hill
- Success and the Self-Image - Zig Ziglar
- The Winning Attitude - John C. Maxwell
- The Learning Centered School - Mike Rutherford
- Victory in Our Schools - John Stafford

# My Personal Power Plan of Action

## *Day One*

Today's Date:_____

**Positive Affirmation Thought for the Day** (write on an index card and carry with you):

### "Every day in every way, I'm getting better and better."

1. **Attitude of Gratitude**: Write the name of one person and something you are grateful for today.
   _____

2. Write the name (or initials) of one person you will listen to and encourage today.
   _____

# *Day Two*

Today's Date:_____

**Positive Affirmation Thought for the Day** (write on an index card and carry with you):

## "People don't care how much I know until they know how much I care."

1.  **Attitude of Gratitude:** Write the name of one person and something you are grateful for today.

    _____

2.  Write the name (or initials) of one person you will listen to and encourage today.

    _____

# *Day Three*

Today's Date:_____

**Positive Affirmation Thought for the Day** (write on an index card and carry with you):

## "In life, I will find exactly what I look for. I will look for the best in people today!"

1. **Attitude of Gratitude:** Write the name of one person and something you are grateful for today.

   _____

2. Write the name (or initials) of one person you will listen to and encourage today.

   _____

# *Day Four*

Today's Date:_____

**Positive Affirmation Thought for the Day** (write on an index card and carry with you):

## "I will get students' best efforts only when I expect their best effort!"

1.  **Attitude of Gratitude:** Write the name of one person and some-thing you are grateful for today.

    _____

2.  Write the name (or initials) of one person you will listen to and encourage today.

    _____

# *Day Five*

Today's Date:_____

**Positive Affirmation Thought for the Day** (write on an index card and carry with you):

## "Someone's opinion of me does not have to become my reality!"

(There is a BIG difference between opinions and reality).

1.  **Attitude of Gratitude:** Write the name of one person and something you are grateful for today.
    _____

2.  Write the name (or initials) of one person you will listen to and encourage today.
    _____

# *Day Six*

Today's Date:_____

**Positive Affirmation Thought for the Day** (write on an index card and carry with you):

## "I will not let the things I cannot do interrupt the things I can do!"

**Note: Before completing the 2 questions below, review your answers from Days 1-5. Continue to be grateful for those already listed and continue to listen to and encourage those you thought of previously.**

1.  Write the name of one person and something you are grateful for today.

    _____

2.  Write the name (or initials) of one person you will listen to and encourage today.

    _____

# *Day Seven*

Today's Date:_____

**Positive Affirmation Thought for the Day** (write on an index card and carry with you):

## "People will know how much I care by how well I listen to them."

**Never underestimate the power of your words and actions. You can change someone's life every day. Why not start today?**

1.  **Attitude of Gratitude**: Write the name of one person and something you are grateful for today.

    _____

2.  Write the name (or initials) of one person you will listen to and encourage today.

    _____

# *Day Eight*

Today's Date:_____

**Positive Affirmation Thought for the Day** (write on an index card and carry with you):

## "Life is 10% what happens to me and 90% what I do about it!"

1. **Attitude of Gratitude:** Write the name of one person and something you are grateful for today.

   _____

2. Write the name (or initials) of one person you will listen to and encourage today.

   _____

# *Day Nine*

Today's Date:_____

**Positive Affirmation Thought for the Day** (write on an index card and carry with you):

## "Only one thing will determine what kind of day I have today— my ATTITUDE! I <u>will</u> have a great day!"

1.  **Attitude of Gratitude:** Write the name of one person and something you are grateful for today.

    _____

2.  Write the name (or initials) of one person you will listen to and encourage today.

    _____

# *Day Ten*

Today's Date:_____

**Positive Affirmation Thought for the Day** (write on an index card and carry with you):

## "Today I will be a dream maker, not a dream breaker!"

1.  Review your previous items listed in Days 1-9 and write the names of the people and things you are **most thankful for**.

    _____
    _____
    _____

2.  Write the names (or initials) of two students you will make a commitment to "connect and care for" the rest of the year— even though you may not want to.

    _____
    _____
    _____

**Suggestion: Along with your reading/listening, complete a Daily Log Book. Simply take a minute to record things such as:**
- *one humorous thing that happened yesterday*
- *one hard-to-reach student I gave an extra effort to yesterday*
- *one thing I am grateful for, etc.*

**Be creative and think of your own personal categories. Have these resources in an easy-to-find place. If you have to "look for it" each morning, unexpected things will happen and it will be difficult to have your "daily quiet time." Make a personal commitment that "no matter what happens" you will make time to mentally prepare yourself for the day. Have an awesome day— every day!**

## References & Recommendations

Someone once said, "There are no 'original' thoughts recorded in any book. Everything that is written has already been thought of by someone else."

I don't know if that statement is true, but I do know every effort has been made to give credit to and recognize individuals whose work contributed to this book. Any omission of a person's name or title of their work is completely unintentional.

# You Can Schedule Jerry King. . .

for an Exciting In-Service Presentation in your School Division or as an Inspirational Keynote Speaker at your next Teacher Conference!

*"We had to move Jerry's presentation at our teacher conference to a large ballroom at the Opryland Hotel in Nashville because over 500 teachers attended! He is an exciting, spellbinding and inspiring speaker who knows how to connect with teachers!"*

**B. Mont Bush, Southern Assoc. of Colleges & Schools (SACS)**

*"As you know, over 700 solemn teachers awaited you for a REQUIRED in-service. The resounding standing ovation that followed your fantastic presentation was indicative of your ability to inspire teachers. What a memorable way to enter the last 25 days of the school year— rejuvenated and ready for the final countdown!"*

**Pat Climer, Supervisor of Instruction**

Limited Dates Available— CALL TODAY!
FREE Speaker Information Packet
4sight Learning
PO Box 108
Galax, VA 24333
(877) 471-1457
email-jking@4sightlearning.com

# "Success Notes & Quotes"

# "Success Notes & Quotes"

# "Success Notes & Quotes"

# "Success Notes & Quotes"

# "Success Notes & Quotes"

# "Success Notes & Quotes"

# "Success Notes & Quotes"

# "Success Notes & Quotes"